Learn
to
Drive Like a Pro

by

Anthony J. Scotti

Learn to Drive Like a Pro
Lessons for
Smart and Skillful Driving
By a Leading
Defensive Driving Trainer

ISBN: 978-0-982-9730-0-4
Library of Congress Control Number: 2011909763

Published by
PhotoGraphics Publishing,
23 Cool Water Court,
Palm Coast, Florida 32137
Phone: 386-246-3672, fax 386-445-7365
www.LearnToDriveLikeAPro.com

About the Author

For 39 years Anthony (Tony) Scotti has catered to the training needs of industry and public service agencies. Today, he is the acknowledged leader in the highly specialized industry of high-risk driving.

He has trained governments, corporations, law enforcement agencies and military organizations to avoid vehicle violence. Going on his fifth decade, his clients include 80% of the Fortune 100. His programs have been conducted in more than 33 countries across five continents. In addition, students from 64 countries have attended Tony Scotti's Vehicle Dynamics courses in the US. Overall, Scotti has conducted more programs in more locations than any other private training institution in the world. Many other security-driver training organizations follow his methods.

Tony has been the subject of numerous interviews in the national media, and has been a speaker at conferences throughout the world. He holds a B. S. in Engineering from Northeastern University and is the author of *Professional Driving Techniques*, PhotoGraphics Publishing and associated teacher's guides that are used in high schools, driving schools and universities across the globe including the university of Beijing, China. He resides in Boston.

He is also the author of *Executive Safety and International Terrorism*, Pearson.

Read more about Tony Scotti at www.securitydriver.com or www.vehicledynamics.net

Acknowledgments

I would like to thank all of the people who made this book possible. Special thanks to the instructors at the Vehicle Dynamics Institute who prove again and again that all this theory works.

Next to my daughter Toni Ann and her husband Larry Snow for their input and support; publisher Joyce Huber; Eleanor and Dennis Eidson, Teddy Giorgio, Kathy Chiariello, Mercedes Benz Corporate Communications; Denise Wilkinson, Shell Oil Company; The National Highway Traffic Safety Administration; Lyndy Lyle Moore, Bike Florida; Anita Liggett, RN and CPR instructor; Maria Shaw; Robin Bartlett, the American Heart Association; Kenneth Liggett, rescue diver; Bryan T. Sammartino, NJ Level II Fire Instructor, Beverly Yevich and Tim Bice.

Over the years I've spent in the driver training/consulting business, I have worked with many top-notch specialists and drivers of all levels and abilities. Though there are too many to mention here individually, the experiences we shared have enriched the pages of this book.

Dedication...

In loving memory of my wife Judy, and

to my daughter Toni-Ann and

grand daughter Sophia

Introduction

Driving like a pro means that you're always in control of your vehicle despite the situations and environment around you. That you always drive smoothly and are always thinking about what you're doing while behind the wheel.

When driving we are constantly confronted with "what if's."

Learn to Drive Like A Pro covers the full spectrum of defensive driving with the "what if's" carefully woven into discussions of the what, whys, and how's of the three parts of the "driving equation" — The Driver, The Vehicle you drive, and The Environment you drive in. It means being at the top of skill level whether you are driving in inclement weather or in rush hour traffic. That's what this book is all about, helping you discover the necessary skills, techniques and mental attitude to become a first rate driver and the enjoyment and sense of pride that comes with that.

The text covers basic to advance driving techniques. The reader will learn everything from how to adjust and use the mirrors properly to the down right exciting, like to how to handle various kinds of skids — braking skids, cornering skids, power skids.

Driving like a pro means operating the vehicle in a manner that will keep you and your passengers safe and secure, but if an emergency develops, you'll be able to handle it with confidence and skill. Emergencies like what to do if a tire blows; or how to make adjustments for driving at night; how to handle basic accident situations involving oncoming cars, entering and merging onto highways, cars ahead; what to do if the car starts to hydroplane, if the accelerator sticks, if the brakes fail; how to figure out safe following distances in varying weather and road conditions and how to use ABS and non-ABS brakes.

Written in an inviting conversational style and filled with abundance of easy-access bulleted lists, driving scenarios, diagrams, and illustrations, it is a book you can pick up, flip through, and — no matter what page you land on — find a useful tip or something to really think about.

Driving like a pro means driving at the highest level, driving at your very best whether motoring along a country road at night, driving to work on an icy road, avoiding a collision at an intersection, or just moving through rush hour traffic on a bright sunny day.

This book will help you become a "Pro Driver." And, I'm sure you'll agree that if more drivers became "Pro Drivers," today's roads would be a much safer place.

Table of Contents

CHAPTER 1

The Walk-Around Checklist

Before getting in and starting the engine:

___Walk completely around the parked vehicle. Make sure children, pets or toys are not under or behind it.

___If your vehicle is equipped with rear viewing, use it when backing up.

___Look over the tires for embedded nails or other sharp objects.

___See that all doors and the trunk are closed tightly

___Clean the windshield of dirt, debris, snow or ice, if needed.

___Clean or defrost the side mirrors, if needed.

___Peer under the car for pools of oil or other vehicle fluids. If you spot any, check under the hood. The engine should be clean and dry. If not, check the oil and transmission fluid.

___Note: Air conditioner condensation is normal in hot climates.

___See that the insurance card, vehicle registration certificate and emergency contact information is in place.

___ Place your cell phone where you can easily find it in an emergency, then TURN IT OFF.

If everything looks fine, hop in.

CHAPTER 2

VEHICLE DYNAMICS

The most important concept to understand is that for a car to perform the four modes of operation (forward travel at a steady speed, accelerating, turning, and braking), it must rely on adhesion between the tire and the roadway.

Tire Adhesion

Tire-to-Road Grip

Automobiles are supported by a cushion of air contained in four flexible rubber tires. If you could place a car on a glass floor and look at it from below, you would see four patches of rubber, each a little smaller than a hand, touching the glass. (see illustration below)

These are the only points of contact between your vehicle and the road. Each of these four small patches of rubber is known as a contact patch and these four tire patches create the traction that makes the car go, stop, and turn.

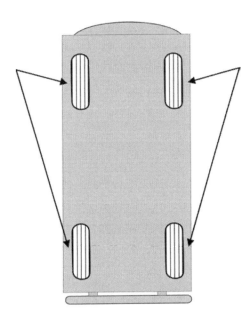

The Limit of Adhesion

The maximum control capacity of the tire patches is called the limit of adhesion. That is the maximum performance available from a particular vehicle and tire design. The limit of adhesion is determined by the grip of the tires to the road, which in turn, is determined by:

> **1.** The vertical force placed on the tire.
>
> **2.** Tire design.
>
> **3.** Condition and type of road surface.
>
> **4.** Vehicle speed.
>
> **5.** Amount of turning force.

Maximum Tire Patch Capability

The four tire patches enable the car to go, or stop, or turn.

In motion, tire patches have a given amount of capability for performing a given action, such as stopping. If that capability is used up, the patch cannot do anything else. There can only be 100% performance from the vehicle.

Rolling Contact

To control a car, rolling contact between tires and the road surface must be maintained. For example, if the tire patches on the two front tires (which are used to steer the car) stop rolling, you lose the ability to steer the car.

- **The steering wheel** does not steer or turn the car; it merely aims the front wheels.
- **Rolling tires** stop the car and turn the car.
- **Front tires** must be rolling in order for the car to turn.

- **Once the tires stop rolling** and start sliding, it is not possible to steer the car.

Rain slicked highways challenge even the most experienced drivers.
Photo © MonkeyBusiness/Dreamstime

CHAPTER 3

Vehicle Equipment

In an accident there are two collisions. The first when the car hits an object, and the second when the occupants hit objects in the car. To prevent serious injury we need to:

1. Keep the people in the car. If a person is ejected from a car the chances of a fatality increase by 300%. Air bags alone won't keep you in the car. The answer is **wear seat belts.**

2. Once the accident occurs, keep the occupants from banging around in the car. **Seat belts and air bags are the difference between life and death.**

3. Absorb some of the energy of the collision.

4. Have and maintain vehicle equipment that will help prevent the incident from happening.

Air Bags save lives. Passenger and driver-side dual air bags are now required in all vehicles sold in the United States. Ideally, the car should also have side air bags. They prevent the driver and passengers from hitting their heads on rigid areas of the vehicle in side impact collisions.

Air Bag Shut-Off Switch - An air bag can injure a child or small adult; ask for a vehicle with an airbag shut-off switch.

Anti-lock Braking System (ABS) is available for nearly all new cars and trucks and is standard equipment on many. If you are buying a truck, check to insure that all four wheels have an ABS.

Back-Up Sensing System – This is a proximity sensor in the rear of the vehicle that senses when the vehicle gets too close to an object and warns the driver. If you are purchasing a mini-vans or SUV consider this for an option.

Rear View Cameras not only protect your car from damage, but also protect children from backing-up accidents. A backup camera is a must in mini vans and SUV's. If you are planning to install a rearview camera select one that turns on automatically whenever the vehicle is put in reverse. If you are doing your own installation, on many vehicles connecting a single wire to the backup light circuit, sends a signal to the rearview camera system, causing it to switch on without any action by the driver. Check the manufacturer's recommendations. High end, multiple-camera systems usually switch on all cameras automatically.

Traction Control (TC) insures maximum contact between the tires and the road. In wet conditions traction control prevents your tires from spinning.

Electronic Stability Control (ESC) uses the existing ABS and traction control computers, plus sensors to monitor what the car is doing after you tell it what to do. Keep in mind that ESC cannot overcome stupidity, it's not a license to drive like an idiot. Researchers found ESC reduces the risk of all single-vehicle crashes by more than 40 percent—fatal ones by 56 percent.

Blind-spot detection/side assist/collision warning technology is designed to alert you to cars or objects in your blind spot during driving or parking, or both.

Lane-departure warning, wake-you-up safety - This is similar to blind-spot/side-assist technology but with more range. It judges an approaching vehicle's speed and distance to warn you of potential danger if you change lanes. It can also warn if it determines your car is wandering out of the lane, which could be useful if you become distracted.

Rollover prevention/mitigation – This is a computer system that is more advanced than electronic stability control system. If the system senses a potential rollover, it will apply the brakes and modulate throttle as needed to help you maintain control.

Emergency brake assist/collision mitigation – A computer system that recognizes when the driver makes a panic stop (a quick shift from gas to brake pedal) and will apply additional brake pressure to help shorten the stopping distance.

Emergency response – Depending on the vehicle, this system turns on interior lighting, unlocks doors and shuts off fuel when air bags deploy. It may also switch on the warning hazards and disconnect the battery terminal from the alternator. Some manufactures alert a response center of the accident and make crash details available to emergency personnel. High consumption electrical components are often shut off.

CHAPTER 4
Car Feel

Keeping in Touch with the Control Limits of the Car

Cars communicate to their drivers in two basic ways, ride and handling. These are two very distinct sensations that are often confused with each other.

Ride

- Ride is the vertical motion of the wheels and tires as they rise and fall over irregularities in the road surface.
- Ride is a comfort factor, one that can be hard or soft.
- A soft riding car smooths out the bumps on the road.
- If a lot of the motion is felt in the cars body and passenger compartment, the result is a hard and frequently uncomfortable ride.
- Many people mistakenly confuse ride with comfort, but ride is just one factor of comfort.
- A car that smooths out all the bumps of the road may be very comfortable, but may not necessarily be a good car for all drivers.

Handling

Handling is the car's ability to remain in control when cornering or being driven through evasive maneuvers. That is its ability to handle various weight transfers. It is also a complicated quality involving the entire driving system.

A study came up with a compromise judgment as to just what can be regarded as satisfactory handling qualities. The results follow.

Be sure to test your brakes before driving over mountain roads.

- Small movements of the wheel should not produce disproportionately large movements of the car.
- The vehicle should follow normal steering inputs correctly and without need of further correction.
- Alternating quick releases of throttle and subsequent braking should not produce unexpected side movements of the car.
- Finally, under varying road irregularities between the left and right sides of the car, and in crosswind conditions, the driver must be able to maintain a straight course easily.

CHAPTER 5

The Mind/Body Driving Connection

What's Involved, What You Need to Know

- Physical and mental conditioning relevant to driving safety
- The signs of physical and mental fatigue
- The problems caused by fatigue
- The danger of over the counter medication
- The role of alcohol and drugs in driver impairment

The Mind/Body Driving Connection It is the foundation of safe driving. If you're driving ability is impaired by illness, injury, fatigue, medications, alcohol or illegal drugs you should seriously consider not driving a vehicle. Physical fatigue can be caused by things you did before you even got into your vehicle. Mental fatigue can cause the same problems as physical fatigue. **How important is physical condition to safe driving?** Consider this scenario:

> You have developed **a shoulder injury**. Thanks to your sore shoulder, it now takes you a little longer to move the steering wheel, say, about one second longer.

> For example, if you are driving along at 40 mph or 58.8 feet per second and suddenly, someone ahead of you runs a stop sign. Because you now take a second longer to react at the wheel, **you also need an additional 60 feet (more or less) to get out of the way.**

Those 60 feet could mean the difference between a wild story to tell at the office or spending years recovering from injury, or worse.

Don't drive while you are emotionally unstable.

Never let your emotions get hold of you while driving. Driving while emotionally upset, especially while unusually angry or sad, can reduce your ability to recognize danger and avoid it.

The solution to avoiding a catastrophe is simple: If anything makes you feel like you can't drive, don't.

If there is any way you can avoid driving, do so. A driver can be in excellent condition and have the eyes of an eagle. But humans, like all other mammals, have a central nervous system, and can get tired. Most drivers, however, often don't think that their fatigue is a serious impediment to their driving ability until the fatigue becomes so serious that they are in real danger.

Physical fatigue can be caused by things you did before you even got into your vehicle.

Driving into work after an all night party may be a memorable experience, but if your condition is such that you have a hard time finding the door handle of the vehicle, you can wind up with an experience you'd rather forget. Sometimes just day to day living such as an all night session with a sick child or other personal emergencies make it impossible to drive bright eyed and bushy tailed.

Mental fatigue can cause the same problems as physical fatigue.

Worries over personal problems, irritation with someone on or off the job who just gave you a hard time — are some of the things that can cause mental fatigue. And, you often don't get an opportunity to take a moment to unwind after a stressful day.

Driving tired or hung over can literally be fatal. You don't have to lead a life of sainthood, but your state of fatigue should never be self induced.

You can resist the effects of fatigue by simply being aware of them, knowing they exist, and being alert to the first warning signs.

The symptoms of fatigue are obvious. After all, everyone has had trouble keeping his or her eyes open at one time or another time. **However, the early signs of fatigue are NOT so obvious.** All of us have had the following experience:

We drive a car down a route we travel every day. Nothing noteworthy happens on the drive, and at some point on the route at an intersection, a bridge, wherever we suddenly realize that we don't recall the drive to that spot. It is as if we suddenly materialized at that spot. This is a strong warning that you are fatigued.

And, if your eyelids are heavy and your eyes are burning, you're definitely fatigued!

Problems While Driving Fatigued

When driving at night, you may have a hard time concentrating on driving. This is no great revelation. When you are tired, you have a difficult time concentrating on anything you do.

When fatigued, you tend to take more risks. You may do things while fatigued you would never think of doing when well rested. Fatigue dulls your mind.

When you're tired, you may have a tough time keeping your car in the proper lane. You may weave side to side and appear drunk, even though you're not. You're just very, very tired. But the results are the same. It's a dangerous, accident producing situation.

When you're fatigued, you often speed up and slow down erratically. If you often find yourself doing that, be aware of it. You're fatigued.

If you're fatigued and you ignore these early warning signals and continue to drive—you develop "tunnel vision." Your vision deteriorates. It gradually becomes very difficult to see. Your attention focuses forward. You will begin to miss signals or signs in the peripheral vision area. This accounts, in part, for many of the accidents that occur near the end of a long day at work.

The surest way to recover from fatigue is to stop and rest or take a short nap.

The most successful driving is performed when the driver rests 20 30 minutes for every one and a half to two hours of driving. The time honored cure of drinking coffee to stay awake is only a stopgap, temporary measure. Sure, the caffeine can bring you up fast, but as the kidneys eliminate it from the body, it will also bring you down fast. Even a brief stop and just a leg stretching short walk can be valuable in fighting fatigue.

Certain groups of people are at a higher risk of suffering from driver fatigue than others. Some of the candidates may surprise you. Do you fit into one or more of these ?

- Professional and over-the-road drivers
- Night-shift workers
- Law enforcement workers
- People who work shifts in excess of 12 hours
- Senior citizens
- Smokers
- People with sleeping disorders

The Way You Sit in a Car Can Help You Remain Alert

There is no single clear cut fool proof way to beat fatigue — but seating position is often critical. Many people blame car seats for an uncomfortable ride. Most of the time the seats aren't to blame — it's the way you sit in them. Sitting erect allows you to stay alert longer. Shoulder and arm positions are also important.

When you get into your vehicle, place your hand at the top of the steering wheel. Your shoulder should be in contact with the seat back. If your shoulder rises off the seat back, you'll find that when you execute an emergency maneuver, you'll be lifted right off your seat. Instead of using the steering wheel to control the car, you'll be using it to hold yourself in place.

Consider the steering wheel as a clock with the top as 12 o'clock and the bottom, six. Ideally, your hands should be at the three and nine o'clock positions. Both hands should remain on the wheel unless it is necessary to operate another control in the car with either hand.

As you sit comfortably, look at your arms. If they are bent at the elbow more than 90 degrees, the result will be poor circulation and very tired arms in a short time.

> **One of the most common errors is sitting too close to the steering wheel. This may indicate a lack of driver confidence, or poor eyesight, or both.**

The opposite extreme, getting too relaxed behind the wheel, can also be a major problem. A driver with the window rolled down, elbow propped up on the sill, and driving with one hand is probably just a little too relaxed and over confident.

Here are some web sites that discuss the problems of fatigue:

www.nhtsa.dot.gov/people/perform/human/drowsy.html

www.trafficsafety.org.

"Avoid Driving While Taking This Product"

All drugs prescription, over the counter, and illegal have the potential to suppress your brain's ability to process information. And the amount of information processing needed to control a vehicle can become more than an impaired brain can handle.

The warning *"Avoid driving while taking this medication"* appears on the back of many over the counter medications and on many prescription bottles. The makers of these medications are trying to tell you something. Even something as mild as a hay fever pill can seriously impair your ability to control a vehicle.

Read the label carefully before you take any medication, and before driving.

If you're taking prescription medication, ask your doctor about the effects it may have on your driving. If it can have any negative effects, do whatever you can to avoid driving while on the medication.

Driving while under the Influence . . .

All tests examining the role of alcohol in driving impairment have indicated the same thing: **alcohol reduces the capacity of the mind to process information from both the road and the overall driving environment.**

Similar tests performed using marijuana showed different results. Although reaction times were slowed by marijuana, they were not slowed as much as when test subjects were given alcohol. The conclusion would seem to be that marijuana is less dangerous than alcohol when it comes to driving. Nevertheless, it is still a dangerous, foolhardy, and illegal thing to do.

What happens when driving under the influence of marijuana is what has been termed a "perceptual failure" — you simply do not see things in time to react to the them. **Put more bluntly, you're so stoned, you don't recognize you're in trouble until it is too late to do anything about it.** There is little research data on marijuana and driving.

Chapter 6
Your Vision and Sense of Space

When driving, the most important aspect of your physical well-being is the quality of your eyesight.

Every action you take behind the wheel is based on eye-hand and/or eye-foot coordination. Although you use all your senses when driving, more than 90 percent of the information you need to control a vehicle comes from what you see.

And, equally important, you need to develop your sense of space while behind the wheel and where your vehicle is in relation to everything around you. You have to develop a questioning attitude that heightens your awareness of both what you can and cannot see.

- You can't avoid an accident if you can't see it coming.
- You can't leave yourself an escape route for every maneuver you make if you aren't aware of the space around you.
- You could potentially cause an accident if you cannot see the road and surroundings well.

PROTECTING YOUR VISION

Even if your eyesight is healthy with or without corrective lenses--hazards such as glare and the low light conditions of night can make seeing difficult for anyone. Even some features of a car's design can hinder your visibility while behind the wheel. A safe driver knows how to protect his vision in all situations.

Seeing at Night

The human eye works far better in daylight than in reduced light conditions. Plainly said, it's hard to see at night.

- Your peripheral vision is decreased.
- Your normally wide field of vision is narrowed to the field of view illuminated by your headlights, the headlights of other vehicles, and fixed road lights.

- When viewed at night, most objects exhibit relatively low contrast, which makes their detection, especially against certain backgrounds, extremely difficult.
- Colors fade at night.
- And your eyes simply need time to adjust to low light conditions before your night vision kicks in and the older you get, the longer this adaptation process takes place.

Night Vision

Dusk and dawn are the two most difficult times of the day for good vision. In the changing light of dawn and dusk, the eye is caught in the middle. At dusk, as the light fades and evening comes on, your eyes gradually adapt to the light and you are given the gift of night vision. But, until that happens, there will be a period of time when you cannot see very well.

At night, if you leave your well-lit house or office and go out and jump into your car and start off, it's the same as when you walk into a movie house after the picture has already started. There you are in a darkened theater, probably juggling an arm load of popcorn and soda, trying to find a seat you simply cannot see. You blunder into a seat, stepping on a few toes on the way, and after a few minutes, you notice how much more light the theater has. Your eyes have had the time they need to adapt to the new lighting situation.

In those first minutes after you jump into your car, you can blunder as badly behind the wheel as you might in a darkened movie theater. In fact, that's one reason people run cars into each other in every imaginable way every day.

Thus, when you plan to drive at night, give your eyes a chance to adjust to the changes in light conditions before you pull out onto the road.

Effects of prolonged daylight exposure on night vision.

Prolonged exposure to glare from sunlight during the day (or, similarly, from headlights at night) can temporarily ruin your night vision, and can lead to eye strain and drowsiness.

To alleviate the effects of such exposure, wear good sunglasses on bright days and take them off as soon as the sun goes down. Also, rest a while before driving at night after a long session of steady daytime driving.

Protecting and Enhancing Your Driving Vision

Eye "protection" against the affects of glare and low-light conditions is important for driving whether or not you normally wear corrective lenses. And, as we'll see, there are some specifications for lenses that make both sunglasses and regular glasses better for driving than others. But regardless of the lens type, all eye wear should provide sufficient lens coverage for peripheral vision, non-obstructive frames and temple pieces, and lightweight, comfortable ear and nose pieces.

Sunglasses

Because the glare of sunlight on bright days can be blinding and too much exposure to sunlight can affect your night vision--**you should always wear sunglasses when driving during daylight hours.** Make sure you wear good-quality sunglasses.

Anti-reflective coating (AR)

If you wear eyeglasses and want to drive at peak efficiency day or night, wear glasses with an anti-reflection (AR) coating on the lenses.

The AR coating does much the same thing as similar coatings on binocular and camera lenses--it increases the lenses efficiency by allowing them to transmit more light. At least eight percent of the light is absorbed within a clear glass lens, but the same lens with an AR coating transmits 99 percent of the light.

Tints

Gray lenses worn during the day provide the right amount of light while properly preparing your eyes for the coming darkness.

After wearing gray lenses all day, your eyes will make the transition to reduced light levels much more readily, and what you see will be a much more accurate picture of what's really happening after dark.

Yellow lenses are recommended for night use because the eye is most sensitive to the yellow portion of the spectrum, and because they effectively increase the apparent viewing brilliance and alleviate 20 percent of usual night-driving fatigue.

Yellow lenses also help on cloudy days, but the effect is usually too brilliant for sunny weather. Adding a yellow tint (for cosmetic purposes) will not reduce the light transmission characteristics of the lenses below 92 percent as long as the lenses are AR coated.

Car Design and Visibility

You can do your part to protect your vision against the glary hazards of day and night driving, but some features of a car's design can actually make visibility difficult at night. And there's not much you can do about it. Be aware of such features and understand how they can affect your ability to see at night.

Tinted glass, which helps keep the interior temperature low during sunny days, also cuts visibility considerably in the dark of night.

Greenish or bluish instrument panel lights are bad for night vision. These colors are at the end of the spectrum to which the eye is least sensitive in low light.

Many cars are equipped with more desirable **red instrument lighting**, a practice that's been common for quite some time in the aircraft industry.

Red light does not interfere with vision outside of the car, and it makes the instruments much clearer to read. Red panel lighting eliminates the endless squinting down at the panel and the need for the eyes to continually readjust from glances at the instruments, or gazes at the road. This does much to reduce overall eye fatigue and makes long night drives more comfortable.

The Myth of "Tired" Eyes

At one time or another all of us have complained of tired eyes. But the eyes themselves do not tire. The nerves, brain, and body fatigue. The heavy eyelids and burning sensation that most people associate with tired eyes are really the physical reactions of a tired body.

If your eyes become "tired" while you're driving, heed the warnings of oncoming fatigue and take the necessary precautions. Don't drive tired!

SELECTIVE VISION AND YOUR SENSE OF SPACE

A great deal of the success of the various safe driving and emergency maneuvers depends on the driver's alertness and powers of observation. You must know what is going on at all times around your vehicle, and you must anticipate what can and might happen. You need space all around your vehicle, because when things go wrong, space gives you time to think and act. And to have space available for when something goes wrong, you need to manage space.

Looking Near, Looking Far

Not looking properly is a major cause of accidents. Don't just base your driving performance on what you can see directly in front of you. All drivers look ahead, but many do not look far enough ahead. Stopping or changing lanes can take a lot of distance, so you must know what the traffic is doing on all sides of you. You must look far enough ahead to be sure you have room to move or stop safely. Perhaps the most important thing to remember is that **you should be able to stop your car within the distance you can SEE.**

Most good drivers look 12 to 15 seconds ahead. That means looking ahead the distance you will travel in 12 to 15 seconds.

At lower speeds, that is about one block; at highway speeds, about a quarter of a mile. If you do not look that far ahead, you may have to stop too quickly or change lanes quickly.

Looking 12 to 15 seconds ahead does not mean not paying attention to closer things. Good drivers shift their attention back and forth, near and far. Look for what could be lurking around corners, on the other side of hills, and moving through intersections.

- Look for vehicles coming onto the highway, into your lane, or turning.
- Watch for brake lights from slow moving vehicles.
- Look for hills, curves, or anything for which you must slow down or change lanes.
- Pay attention to traffic signals and signs. If a light has been green for a long time, it will probably change before you get there. Start slowing down and be ready to stop. Traffic signs may alert you to road conditions where you may have to change speed.

By seeing these things far enough ahead, you can change your speed or change lanes if necessary to avoid a problem.

Always Leave Yourself an "Out"

One of the basic points about avoiding accidents is easy to understand and very fundamental to safe driving: **Leave yourself an out** or escape route for every move you make.

To do this, you must **be aware of what's going on around you at all times.** Your best tools for doing this are your mirrors, both rearview and side view. (Too many of us only use our rearview mirrors when we want to pull out into traffic.)

Use all your mirrors in order to see the big picture. You need accurate information about what's going on your right, left, and rear.

In an emergency situation, such as a collision right in front of you, you need all the information you can get about what's happening around you, and you need it fast. Mirrors are your best way of getting this information.

(See Windshields and Mirrors for tips on how to properly adjust and use your vehicle's mirrors.)

Sense of Space in Traffic Situations

Its hard to avoid traffic. All of us have to drive in traffic. Its impossible to avoid, so we learn to live with it. It's a fact of life.

In heavy, stop-and-go traffic, its vital to pay attention to what's going on around you. That can be tough because, from minute to minute, it may not seem like much is happening, especially if the traffic isn't moving very fast.

Keep your eyes and mind focused on the tasks in front of you. Maintain a safe distance from the car in front of you.

Be watchful for cars pulling out of parking spots. Many do so without looking where they are heading.

Watch out for the distracted person, the one with the cell phone, map or the one trying to read directions on his GPS screen or Ipad® instead of looking where he's going.

And there's another kind of traffic one that's even more deadly— high-speed traffic. This is traffic bunched together and moving at high speed. Cars are being driven very fast, very close to one another. There's not much you can do about this. **Try to give all the vehicles around you as much space as you can.**

CHAPTER 7
Windshield and Mirrors
Your windows to the outside world

WINDSHIELD

Windshield Visibility

A non-tinted windshield permits 89 percent of the perpendicular light to pass through. The rule is that the windshield needs to pass only 70 percent of the light to meet safety standards.

- Clear away the fog
- Clear vision is the foundation of safe driving.

Keep a clean rag or paper towels and some windshield cleaner in your car for times like this. Photo © Magicshapes/Dreamstime

Streaks and smears on a windshield may produce kaleidoscopic effects when lights shine on them at night. Photo © Alleks/Dreamstime

Windshield

The most important safety feature is right in front of your eyes.

Streaks and smears on windshields can produce extremely disorienting kaleidoscopic effects when lights shine on them at night. If your windshield is really filthy, wash it with soap and water first, then clean it again with window cleaner. If you still have water spots or streaks, very gently wipe the glass with 00 steel wool in circular motions.

Setting up Your Mirrors

Let's look at how to use the mirrors and how to adjust the mirrors.

Start with the right side mirror (Zone 1 – see illustration next page). Adjust it so it gives a clear view of traffic on your right.

It must be adjusted so you can see a vehicle or part of the vehicle on the right until your peripheral vision picks up the vehicle on the right. Therefore, as the vehicle leaves your vision in the rear view mirror, it must appear in the right side mirror.

24

Mirror Zones

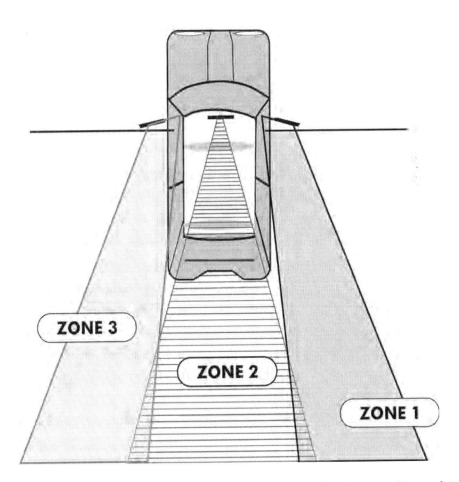

ZONE 3

ZONE 2

ZONE 1

As it leaves Zone One & Two it must appear in your peripheral vision. Now adjust the center mirror (rear view mirrors) on your vehicle (Zone 2). The center mirror will cover everything directly behind you, but it also covers the blind spot on your right that your right mirror failed to pick up.

It must also cover part of the left side of the vehicle where you will also have a blind spot on the left mirror.

The rear view mirror must be adjusted so that as a vehicle disappears from its view it will appear in one of the side mirrors (Zone One or Zone Three).
Now adjust the left mirror (Zone 3); adjust it so you can see a vehicle coming up on your left side and keeps it in view until your peripheral vision picks it up.

Why is it so important to know if a car is coming up behind you? When you have to make an evasive action, you need to know what's behind you and what may inhibit a move either left or right.

When the vehicle leaves the rear view mirror (ZONE TWO) it must appear in the left side mirror (ZONE THREE). When it leaves the left side mirror it must appear in the driver's peripheral vision.

Every driver should be cognizant of what is in their mirrors every few seconds; traffic changes — so does your escape routes. Remember, well adjusted mirrors will give you up-to-date information every few seconds. Properly adjusted mirrors could give you the emergency time you need to avoid an accident.

CHAPTER 8
Starting the Engine & Fuel Efficiency

You probably don't think much about how to start your car. You get in, turn the key, and go-until the day the car balks. Knowing the right way to start your car, though, will lengthen your engine's life, reduce repair bills, and reduce frustration by making your car start more willingly. Follow these steps for "cold starts," that is, starting your car for the first time in the morning, or when the engine is at ambient temperature- the temperature outside.

On carburetor cars, if the temperature is below freezing or if the engine hasn't been started in at least two days: **Press the gas two or three times to make the initial fuel mixture "richer"**-that is, to increase the proportion of gas in the gas-air combination.

Fuel-injected cars are computer controlled, so you shouldn't touch the gas pedal at all. "In fact," "hitting the gas only confuses the computer."

Finally, turn the key. **Don't press or pump the gas pedal while turning the key in a fuel-injected car.** In a carbureted car, press the accelerator down to one-quarter to one half of the way. Release the gas immediately when the car starts.

In normal weather the car should start in four seconds. At temperatures below freezing, the car should start in 10 seconds.

Release the key from start position as soon as the car starts. Do not crank the car for more than 30 seconds, or the starter motor may overheat.

No matter what kind of car you have, fuel-injected or carbureted, automatic or manual, you don't need a warm up. **Once the engine starts, drive off gently. If you can't, you need repairs.**

Long warm-ups reduce gas mileage, and long periods at fast idle (10 minutes or more) will damage the catalytic converter. On the other hand, avoid putting undo stress on the engine until the oil has had the opportunity to circulate to all engine parts.

Never race any engine right after starting no matter how impatient you are to "warm it up." Ninety percent of all engine wear occurs during the first few minutes.

Release the ignition if the car doesn't start on the first try. Let the car sit for a few seconds and try again. If it still doesn't start, wait several minutes before trying again.

If the engine should flood press the accelerator down all the way to

Release the ignition if the car doesn't start on the first try.

Photo © Joyce Huber

the floor and hold it. On a fuel-injected car this sends a message to the computer that the car is flooded, and the computer in turn shuts off all fuel.

On a carburetor equipped car, pressing the accelerator all the way to the floor allows more air to pass through the manifold, evaporating the excess gas. Don't pump the accelerator while you crank the engine.

Fuel Efficiency

To get the most for your money at the fuel pump, fill your vehicle's gas tank in the early morning when the ground temperature is still cold.

A one degree rise in temperature is a big deal in the business, but the service stations do not have temperature compensation at the pumps. All service stations have their storage tanks buried beneath the ground. The colder the ground the denser the fuel, when it gets warmer petrol expands, so if buying in the afternoon or evening your gallon is not exactly a gallon.

Pump the gas slowly. The gas nozzle trigger has three stages; low, middle and high. If you are pumping on the fast rate, some of the liquid that goes into your tank becomes vapor. Those vapors are being sucked up and back into the underground storage tank so you're getting less worth for your money.

Fill up when your tank is HALF FULL. The more fuel you have in your tank, the less air occupies its empty space. Petrol evaporates faster than you can imagine. In fact, petroleum storage tanks have an internal floating roof that allows zero clearance between petrol and the atmosphere to minimize evaporation.

CHAPTER 9

Taking to the Road

If you start the day from a garage or driveway your first driving task may be backing out to the road. **To gain proficiency in reverse, you must keep in mind that cars are designed to go forward.**

Caster, the force that helps to straighten out the front wheels after turning a corner, also gives the car stability while traveling forward. Unfortunately, this stabilizing forward force de-stabilizes the car while it's in reverse. The steering wheel will not center automatically if you loosen your grip on it, as it will when in forward motion. Small changes in steering wheel movement cause big changes in the way the car reacts to your inputs. The faster you go in reverse, the more difficult control becomes.

Photo © Eli Haber

Key Points When Backing Up

- **No matter how short the distance you wish to travel in reverse, look where you're going and drive slowly.** Most cars feature a blind spot or spots to the rear large enough to hide a small child.
- Blow your horn.
- But whatever you do, be absolutely sure there **is no one behind you when you back up.**
- **Before you put the car in reverse, make sure the area in front of the car is clear.** Some cars have long hoods and broad front ends. As you maneuver backwards and turn, the noses of many large cars swing out to the side dramatically and you could hit something — or someone. Many cars in America today have badly dented fenders because drivers neglected to perform this check.
- **Try not to back into an intersection that contains a lot of traffic.**
- **Make sure you are able to reach all your car's controls.** It's a little foolish to hike yourself up in the seat for good visibility, put the car into reverse, then discover you can't reach the brake pedal!

- If you're **backing up to the right,** look over your right shoulder.
- Short people have a hard time backing up because they have a hard time seeing over the back of the front seat and out the rear window. Seat cushions made for driving are available in auto stores, truck stops and discount stores with automotive departments. Besides comfort, they will sit you a little higher.
- **Make sure the car has come to a complete halt before you put it in reverse.**
- **Keep a foot on the brake while putting the car in reverse.**
- Another problem with backing up is knowing what to do with the steering wheel.
- **Move the top of the steering wheel in the direction you wish the car to move.** It's actually no different from what you do while driving forward.
  Never combine a great deal of steering wheel movement with a heavy foot on the gas pedal. You will surely lose control of the car. Instead, use smooth applications of the brake, steering wheel, and accelerator.

Backing up a Trailer

When backing up a trailer or other towed vehicle, place your hand on the bottom of the steering wheel and turn the wheel in the direction that you want the trailer to go.

Like riding a bicycle, backing up a trailer with precision is a coordination effort that can be daunting at first. Skill comes only with practice. Without mastering the skill you encounter a situation where the trailer seems to have a will of its own. Over controlling in the wrong direction may even result in a jack knife situation where the trailer doubles back until it's touching the tow vehicle.

The buddy or spotter system works best in practice and learning. Find an empty country lane or parking lot if you live in a city. Pick an alert buddy that you can depend on. Agree on hand signals before you start or, better yet, borrow a pair of walkie talkies.

Success depends greatly on the quality of your rear vision. You can't back up safely if you can't see where you're going. **For maximum vision, adjust the side view mirrors so you can see the rear corners**

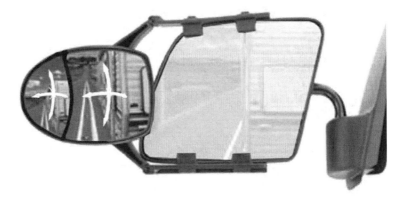

Reese Duel View Mirrors clip on existing side view mirrors. They are available for around $25 each through www.reese-hitches.com Photo courtesy Reese Hitches.

of your trailer. If your mirrors don't extend out enough, consider purchasing a set of large extended mirrors with convex areas. Or pick up a set of adjustable, clip-on convex mirrors such as Reese™ Duel View, available at online at www.reese-hitches.com or Sears®. The flat inside mirror provides the rear view while the clip-on convex acts as a blind spot mirror.

- **Find a large empty lane or parking lot to practice in.**
- **Pick an area away from cars, trees, fire hydrants, ditches and things you don't want to impact.**
- **Make certain you can see and hear your buddy at all times.**
- **Place your hand at the bottom of the steering wheel (six o'clock position), and gently turn it in the direction you want the trailer to end up.** If it pivots in the wrong direction, turn the wheel gently in that direction. (see illustration next page).

First practice backing up in a straight line. Pull forward to have the tow vehicle and trailer in a straight line. Back up slowly. If it's not going where you want it, pull forward, straighten it out and try again. Keep in mind the tow vehicle will turn left when you turn the steering wheel to the right. The easiest method is to place your hand on the bottom of the steering wheel. Thus, when you move your hand to the right or left the trailer turns the same way. Make small adjustments in turning and acceleration till you get it right.

Once you master backing up in a straight line, then try along a curve. Set up cones, if available.

If you're not sure you're going exactly where you expect, put the vehicle in park and get out and look.

After gaining skill with backing up straight, then along a curve, try parallel parking–with traffic cones. Once you've gained skill in parking, you can confidently take to the road.

Turn the wheel opposite of the way you want the trailer to turn when backing up.

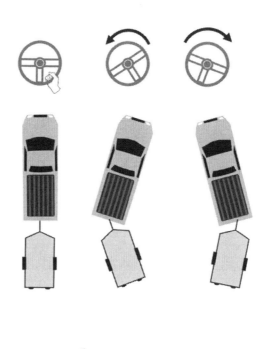

CHAPTER 10

TURNING AROUND

There are three ways to reverse direction - U-turns - Two-point turns - Three-point turns

U-turns

Stop as close to the right side of the road as possible.
Look both ways before you even begin to turn the steering wheel and start the turn.
Let everyone around you know what you're going to do. Use your left-turn signal to indicate what you're planning.
When you're certain that everyone has been notified, **turn the wheel as quickly as possible and as sharply as necessary**, and complete the turn.
Before pulling out make sure to **look over your shoulder and check for oncoming traffic.**

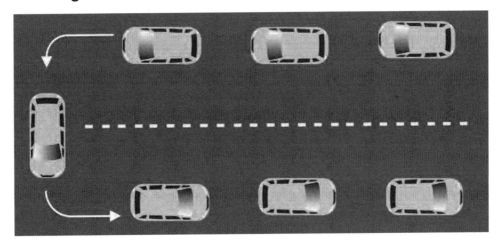

TWO-POINT TURNS

A right side two-point turn

A right-side, two-point turn requires you to stop the car, back it into a road or driveway on the right side of the highway, and drive out onto the highway and make your turn.

Signal your intention to stop the car – before you move backwards, check to make sure that the path behind you is clear - Before re-entering the traffic again, make sure you can do so safely..

A Left-Side Road Turn

The left-hand turn requires the driver to drive nose-first into a road or driveway on the left side of the road, then back onto the highway, straighten out, and drive off.

Signal your intention to stop and to make a left-hand turn onto the side road or driveway. The most dangerous moment in this turn is when you're backing into on-coming traffic.

Watch out for this oncoming flow, and make sure all is clear in front of you before moving out into the traffic.

The Three-Point Turn

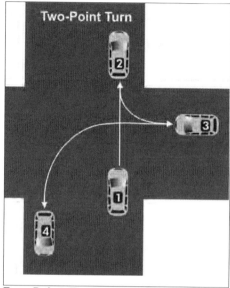

Two Point Turn (shown above) is useful when the road is too narrow, or restricted visibility does not permit a U-turn, or a U-turn is illegal.Two point turn.jpg

The three-point turn should be made only where there is no other choice.

First pull over and get as close to the right side of the road as possible - Turn your car as though you were going to do a U-turn.

Just before the front wheels of your car reach the far side of the road, turn the steering wheel to the right, check ahead and behind for oncoming traffic, put the car in reverse, and back up across both lanes - Remember: Whenever the car is moving backwards, you should be looking the same way. Just prior to reaching the other side of the road, turn the wheel to the left.

TURNING AT INTERSECTIONS

Turning Left at Intersections

- **Be sure there is enough space to turn left.**
- **Signal your intent to turn.**
- **If there are two left turn lanes, take the right-hand turn lane.**
- **Start to turn only after you are sure your vehicle's rear will clear the center line.**

- **Watch your vehicle's progress in the side mirrors. Steer the vehicle wide of the lane, if necessary.**

When the vehicle's wheels are into the lane, **steer left to put the vehicle in the lane and straighten up.**

Turning Right at Intersections

- **Make sure there is enough space to turn right**
- **Signal to turn at least 100 feet ahead of the intersection**, and slow down gradually as you approach the turn.
- **Be sure to let oncoming traffic clear before you make your turn.**
- **Stay as close as possible to the right edge of the road or street.** Never swerve to the left before turning right.
- Position your vehicle in the right-hand lane. **Keep your vehicle's rear close to the curb**
- **Do not turn wide to the left as you start the turn** or the driver behind you might think you are turning left.
- **Pull forward into the intersection past the right corner.** Do this so the rear wheels can clear the curb.
- **Check your progress** using the right side mirrors.
- **Watch for oncoming cars** if are swinging wide into the left or oncoming lane.

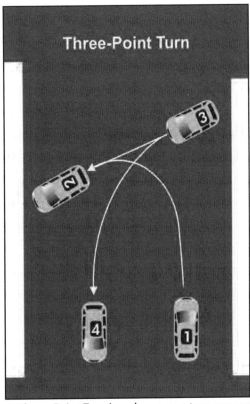

Three-Point Turn

A Three-Point Turn is a dangerous turn-around that should not be used unless there is no other way of changing direction.

CHAPTER 11

Stopping the Car

The first thing we need to know is that brakes don't stop cars. Brakes stop wheels from rolling. The friction of the tires against the road surface stops car.

Most drivers realize that the higher the car's speed, the more distance required to stop. What is surprising to many drivers is how much additional distance it takes to stop a vehicle with just a small increase in speed.

- **Doubling your speed you increases your stopping distance by a factor of four.**
- If you increase speed from 40 to 44 mph, speed has increased by 10% but stopping distance has increased by 20%.
- If you increase speed from 40 to 50 mph, speed has increased by 25% but stopping distance has increased by 50%.
- In an emergency situation with ABS brakes, apply your brakes hard and stay on them. **You should not pump the brake pedal at any time on an ABS system**
- Hard application of ABS brakes will cause the brake pedal to vibrate or pulsate. Don't let the vibration bother you. **The pedal is supposed to vibrate.**
- Along with the vibration, **you will hear a strange groaning noise.** It is supposed to make that noise, and a periodic decrease in brake pedal pressure may occur.
- **Many times the driver's eyes fixate on the object they are trying to avoid, and the result is they drive into it.**
- In an emergency, it's all about where you look while the emergency is unfolding. Simply stated – **your hands go where your eyes look. As soon as the emergency presents itself look for a place to put the vehicle.**

CHAPTER 12

Passing Another Vehicle

Safe passing depends mainly on your knowing three things:

1. When to pass

2. When not to pass

3. How to pass safely

Before passing another vehicle take note, is the car you are about to pass aware of your presence? Are there side roads ahead that may hide a car about to turn into your path? Even if you can't see them, assume they're there.

Consider how long is all this going to take? Do you have enough time to pass and get back in your lane? Estimating whether or not the pass is safe requires quick thinking.

Check your mirrors before you pass; it's just good sense to check your mirrors before you make any move with your car.

When you pull out to pass do not speed up directly behind a vehicle and then turn out suddenly just before you get to it.

Also, the closer you are to the vehicle in front of you the harder it is to see around them. You cannot pass safely unless you can see far enough ahead to be sure that you can get back in line before you meet any traffic coming from the opposite direction.

Your best friend here is your own good sense and your experience as a good driver. But if you have to make a mistake, make it on the side of too much caution, instead of not enough.

WHEN NOT TO PASS

When it comes to passing, there are some NEVERS — situations where passing is always dangerous or unlawful:

- *Never* pass when you cannot see that the left side of the road is free of oncoming traffic far enough ahead to pass safely.
- *Never* pass on any curve or hill where you cannot see 500 feet.
- *Never* pass at night when you can't see far ahead.
- *Never* pass unless you have sufficient distance to pass and return to the right without coming within 100 Ft of an approaching vehicle.
- *Never* pass at an intersection.
- *Never* pass when there is a single or double solid line between lanes or when your lane's side of a double line is solid.
- *Never* pass at crosswalks where a vehicle has stopped to allow a pedestrian to cross.
- *Never* pass a stopped school bus with its warning flashers on.
- *Never* pass another vehicle on curves.
- *Never* pass another vehicle at intersections
- *Never* pass another vehicle when crossing railroad tracks.
- *Never* pass another vehicle at night when you can't see far ahead.

HOW TO PASS SAFELY

Signaling Your Intent to Pass

- Look ahead and behind to be sure it is safe to pass.
- Signaling the driver AHEAD of you
- Let the driver of the vehicle ahead know what you intend to do. She may be ready to pass the vehicle ahead of her or to turn left.
- Blow your horn as a signal to her. The horn signal is required by law in most localities, and it puts the driver of the vehicle being passed under a legal obligation to help you pass.
- At night, give the driver ahead an additional signal by flashing your headlights from low to high beam and back to low. However, do not use the light signal as a substitute for the horn signal.

Signaling the driver BEHIND you

The driver of the vehicle behind you also needs to know what you are going to do. He may be pulling out to pass you.

- Give a left-turn signal when you are about to pull out to pass.

Safe Passing Distance

You cannot pass safely unless you can see far enough ahead to be sure that you can get back in line before you meet traffic coming from the opposite direction. You must also be able to get back into line before meeting any traffic crossing or turning onto the road on which you are driving.

But how far ahead is far enough? Give yourself and the driver of the vehicle you are passing plenty of room.

Start to pass from a safe following distance. If the vehicle you want to pass is traveling at 30 mph, start from at least 60 feet behind it. Do not speed up directly behind a vehicle and then turn out suddenly just before you get to it.

A driver who tailgates does not give himself enough time or distance to handle emergency situations. Tailgating interferes with your view of the road ahead. The other driver may slow down or stop, and he can do so much more quickly than you can because his speed is lower. If he does, you will almost certainly be unable to slow down or stop in time. If you try to avoid a collision by turning sharply aside, you may skid off the road, turn over, or smash into another vehicle.

41

- Drift over to the left and speed up quickly.
- As you go by another vehicle, be sure there is plenty of distance between the right side of your vehicle and the left side of the other vehicle. The law in most localities requires a minimum clearance of two feet.

You have not finished passing until you get back onto your own side of the road or in the lane where you belong, leaving the vehicle you have just passed at a safe following distance behind you.

For example, if the vehicle you are passing is traveling at 30 mph, leave 60 feet clear before returning to your own side of the road (20 feet for every 10 mph of speed).

If you force the driver of the vehicle you have just passed to slow down as you get back into line, you have not passed safely.

Of course, it is difficult to see the vehicle you have just passed and estimate the distance. A good rule of thumb is to return to the right side of the road when you can see the vehicle you have passed in your rearview mirror.

As a general rule, do not attempt to pass more than one vehicle at a time. Passing several vehicles increases the danger because it increases the time you spend and the distance you cover while out of your own lane.

If you come up behind a long line of vehicles, you can almost be sure that every driver except the first one is waiting for an opportunity to pass. The safe and courteous thing to do is to wait your turn.

On the other hand, if you are behind a slow-moving vehicle, it is discourteous to the drivers behind you not to pass when you have the opportunity.

SAFE PASSING SPEEDS

And just how fast should you pass someone? Neither too fast, nor too slow. But how fast is too fast? And how slow is too slow?

For example: Suppose that you want to pass a vehicle that is traveling at 30 mph. You would have to travel whatever distance it travels while you are passing, plus an additional distance besides. Since the other vehicle's speed is 30 mph, the additional distance in this case would be about 160 feet.

It is generally a good idea to pass at a speed at least 10 to 15 mph faster than the speed of the vehicle being passed.

If your speed is only 5 mph faster, it will take you twice the time and almost twice the distance to completely pass the other vehicle. On the other hand, there is no point in passing at too fast a speed. In passing at 20 mph faster instead of 15 mph faster than the speed of the vehicle being passed, the advantage amounts to only 1 or 2 seconds gained. It is usually offset by the danger of increased speed.

If too much increased speed is required to pass and return to your lane, the wise decision is not to pass.

Similarly, when the driver ahead of you is traveling just under the speed limit, the safest thing to do is forget about passing.

For example: Suppose that you want to pass a vehicle traveling at 50 mph when the speed limit is 55 mph. In this case, driving your vehicle 10 to 15 mph faster would be unlawful because passing is no excuse for exceeding the speed limit. Yet if you pass at 55 mph, you will need 2,640 feet or exactly half a mile to pass the other vehicle.

So, the best thing to do is settle down behind him at a safe following distance. You may reach your destination a few minutes later than if you had attempted to pass, but at least you will not have broken the law.

SPECIAL PASSING SITUATIONS

Passing on Three-Lane Highways

Passing on a three-lane highway demands extra caution.

- Do not pass except in the center lane, and then only when the center lane is marked for passing in your direction. In some cases, the center lane may be so marked that it is open for passing in both directions.
- Before passing, make sure that none of the vehicles coming from the opposite direction are moving out to pass.
- Never use the center lane to pass if your view of the road ahead is obstructed by a hill or curve.

The one exception to using only the center lane for passing is that you may pass in the right lane if the vehicle in the center lane is making a left turn.

PASSING ON THE RIGHT

Passing on the right, except as noted above, is usually dangerous and unlawful. It puts you on the other driver's blind side. He may be intending to make a right turn or to pull over to the right side of the road. In either case, an accident is almost certain.

There are, however, three situations in which passing on the right is usually permissible and reasonably safe:

- If the highway has at least two lanes going in each direction.
- If all lanes of traffic move in the same direction (one-way street).
- If the vehicle you are passing is in a left-turn lane.

BEING PASSED

When being passed, the law requires you to help the other driver get by.

Give Way to the Right

When the driver of the passing vehicle blows his horn, you must do one thing — give way to the right.

Even if you are already on your own side of the road, move over as close as safety will permit to the right-hand edge of the road.

Maintain a Steady Speed

When you are being passed, it is usually safest to maintain a steady speed. By doing this, you allow the passing driver to judge passing distance with greater accuracy. If you slow down, you may mislead the passing driver into overestimating his speed.

The law does not permit you to increase your speed when you're being passed. Speeding up forces the passing driver to cover more distance and take more time to get by you. It exposes both of you to unnecessary danger.

If an attempt to pass you becomes dangerous, you may be able to make it safer for everyone by slowing down and allowing the passing vehicle to get back into the proper lane in less time and distance.

If, however, you see that a driver is trying to get back into line behind you, rather than ahead of you, do not slow down. In this case, it is much safer to speed up a little to give him more room.

When danger develops in passing, do not stand on your rights. Use all driving skills to avoid an accident.

PASSING IN AN SUV

When driving an SUV you need to leave a lot of room between you and the car you are about to pass. The reason for this is placarded over the visor of most SUV's. "Avoid turning the wheel sharply" If you pull up to close to the vehicle in front of you, that's exactly what you will have to do.

IN ANY VEHICLE

When you have completed the pass be sure there is plenty of distance between the right side of your vehicle and the left side of the other vehicle.

Return to the right side of the road when you can see the vehicle you have passed in your rearview mirror.

Chapter 13

Under Steer and Over Steer
Understanding the Basics

The phrases **Understeer** and **Oversteer** are often used to explain vehicle characteristics. They describe what happens to a vehicle when you move the controls, specifically the steering wheel.

When you turn the steering wheel there is energy pushing on the **Center of Gravity** (CG) of your vehicle, and it makes no difference what you are driving or where you are driving it. The laws of physics dictate that when you move the steering wheel, you create a force acting on the CG of the vehicle. The amount of energy (As mentioned above it can be measured in G's or in pounds) is determined by how much you move the steering wheel and how fast you're traveling.

It's pretty simple, the more speed and the more steering, the more energy pushing on the vehicle. Remember from high school science "for every action there is an opposite and equal reaction." Thus, if there is a force pushing on the CG of your vehicle, there has to be an equal and opposite force pushing back. That force pushing back is created by friction your tires make with the road.

If you drove around a corner or made an emergency maneuver that created 3200 lbs pushing on the CG of your vehicle - in the perfect world your tires would be pushing back 1600 lbs front and rear. This would be called **neutral steering,** and it is a characteristic seldom found in vehicles.

But what happens most often is either oversteer or understeer.

Understeer (NASCAR guys call this "push") in a turn, or emergency maneuver **is the condition where the front tires lose adhesion while the rear tires remain in contact with the pavement.** The car tends to travel straight ahead, even though you are turning the wheel. For example, the front tires might only push back with 1000 lbs and the back tires push back with 1600 lbs.

Each vehicle is designed to withstand — or absorb — only so much of these forces before it becomes unstable. Thus, it is not only important for you to understand how the various combinations of your vehicle's speed and weight and forces affect your ability to control your car, you must also understand the **control limits** that are designed into your particular vehicle. To do this, you have to follow a two-step process:

Understeer, You aim at A, but arrive at B   **Oversteer**. You aim at A, but arrive at B

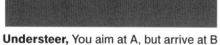

First you have to figure out the G-force (a unit of force equal to the force exerted by gravity) that is created by your handling of the vehicle — how much you step on the gas pedal and how sharply you turn the steering wheel.

Then you have to compare the amount of G-force generated with the amount of your vehicle was designed to absorb (it's G rating) before it would become unstable — and you'd lose control.

Understanding these forces and control limits should give you an intuitive understanding of how you can better handle your vehicle.

THE BASICS

In an under steering condition turning the steering wheel more won't work and will aggravate the scenario. To fix it reduce speed and/or reduce the amount the steering wheel is turned. **You can correct understeer by reducing throttle until the front tires regain adhesion.**

Oversteer (NASCAR guys call this "loose") — In a turn, or emergency maneuver oversteer is the condition where your rear tires lose adhesion while your front tires remain in contact with the pavement. The back end of your car tends to slide out. Turning the steering wheel more will makes things worse.

To fix oversteer reduce speed and turn the steering wheel in the opposite direction of the skid. In our example the rear tires can push back with only 1000 lbs and the fronts push back with 1600 lbs.

Correcting oversteer can be tricky and requires training and practice. Then there is something called **power oversteer.**

An example of power oversteer; you're driving fast around a corner - as you exit the corner you apply gas, and the back of the vehicle starts to swing out. The back of the vehicle is swinging out because you have applied too much gas and the back tires are loosing adhesion - to correct the problem you either have to steer less or give it less gas.

Also there is another form of oversteer that is called **trailing throttle oversteer,** which means that as you turn and take your foot off the gas the back of the car swings out. Trailing throttle oversteer is due to the back tires doing funky things when you transfer weight from the rear to the front. (Very common in armored vehicles). Correct trailing-throttle oversteer by smoothly increasing the throttle (to transfer weight to the rear tires) and apply steering to counter the rotation.

Chapter 14
TRACTION AND WEIGHT TRANSFER
Maintaining Traction:

Tire-to-Road Grip and Weight Transfer

The most important concept to understand in vehicle dynamics is that for a car to perform the four modes of operation (forward travel at a steady speed, accelerating, turning, braking), it must rely on adhesion between the tire and the roadway.

Tire Adhesion — Tire-to-Road Grip

Automobiles are supported by a cushion of air contained in four flexible rubber tires. If you could place a car on a glass floor and look at it from below, you would see four patches of rubber, each a little smaller than a hand, touching the glass. These are the only points of contact between your vehicle and the road. (See illustration)

Each of these four small patches of rubber is known as a contact patch and these four tire patches create the traction that makes the car go, stop, and turn. (They are also the sources of the control feedback you receive from the car. (See "Car Feel" chapter)

The "Limit of Adhesion"

The maximum control capacity of the tire patches is called the limit of adhesion. This limit is the maximum performance available from a particular vehicle and tire design. The limit of adhesion is determined by the grip of the tires to the road, which in turn is determined by:

- The vertical force placed on the tire.
- Tire design.
- Condition and type of road surface.
- Vehicle speed.
- Amount of turning force.

The maximum amount of acceleration, braking, and cornering (steering) forces possible with a given set of tires are all determined by this tire-to-road grip. Although there is a limit to what a car and its given set of tires can do, we sometimes force a car to exceed those limits by over accelerating, over-steering, over-braking. And, if you do try to force a car to go beyond those limits especially beyond the limit of adhesion you will go out of control.

Maximum tire patch capability for performing a given action

The four tire patches enable the car to go, or stop, or turn. In motion, tire patches have a given amount of capability for performing a given action, such as stopping. If that capability is used up in a given action, then the patch cannot do anything else.

There can only be 100% performance from the vehicle if the environment allows it. If the driver uses 100% to stop, the car will not turn. If the driver uses 100% to turn, the car will not stop. If the driver uses 60% to stop, he can use 40% to turn.

If the driver tries to use more than 100% by applying too much braking and too much steering, the driver will lose control of the vehicle.

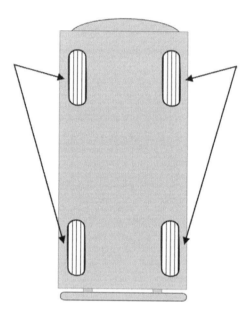

Tire Adhesion: Four Patches of Rubber. Each patch is a little smaller than a hand. The tire patches are the only points of control between your vehicle and the road.

This all assumes that the environment allows the driver to use 100%. If the environment only allows 50%, then the driver will be able to use only 50% of the vehicle's capability.

Rolling Contact

To control a car, rolling contact between tires and the road surface must be maintained. If, for example, while you're driving along, something happens or some-

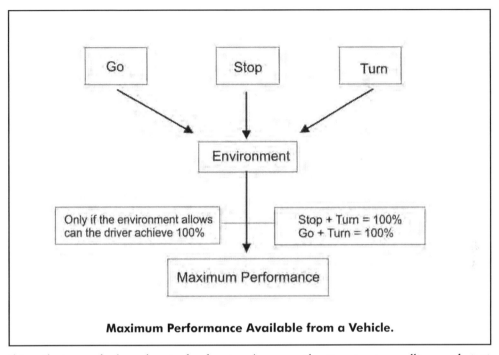

Maximum Performance Available from a Vehicle.

thing that you do (accelerate, brake, turn) causes the tires to stop rolling and start spinning without traction or sliding outright, life gets exciting in a hurry.

If, for example, the tire patches on the two front tires (which are used to steer the car) stop rolling for any reason, you lose the ability to steer the car. Therefore, we are correct when we say **the steering wheel does not steer or turn the car; it merely aims the front wheels.**

Rolling tires stop the car and turn the car. Front tires must be rolling for the car to turn. To put it in simpler terms, rolling friction is greater than sliding friction. Once the tires have stopped rolling and started sliding it is not possible to steer the car.

Although it is important to understand what makes tires develop traction, its far more important to understand what causes cars to lose traction and go out of control.

Weight Transfer to the Tire Patches

Weight transfer problems develop when a driver applies too much steering and braking force, or too much power and too much steering. The result in both cases

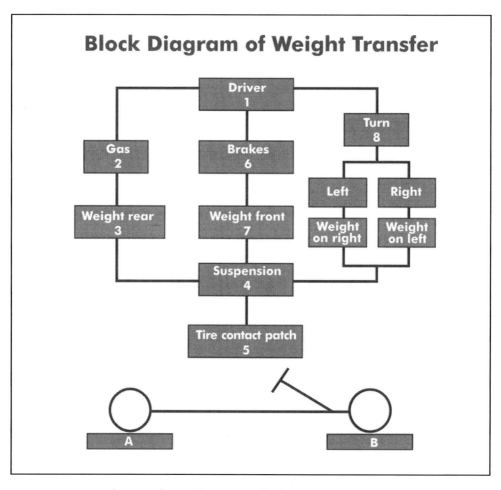

Block Diagram of Weight Transfer

is excessive weight transfer to the tires, which, in turn, puts too much pressure on the tire patches. Too much weight on the tire patches causes the driver to lose control.

Anytime you move a vehicle control (gas pedal, brake pedal, or steering wheel), you are transferring weight through the car's suspension system to the tire patches. If these forces produce stresses on the tires greater than they can accept, those tires reach their limit of adhesion and let go. Again, the vehicle is out of control.

Referring to the *Block Diagram of Weight Transfer* above, you can easily see how weight transfers to the rear, front, left, or right depending on a driver's actions and how excessive weight transfer can cause loss of control.

Weight transfer to the rear

The driver (Square 1) presses down on the gas pedal (Square 2). If we could put scales under the front and back wheels of the car when the gas pedal is depressed, we would see that the weight on the rear scale (A) increases and the weight on the front scale (B) decreases.

In acceleration, weight was transferred from the front to the rear of the car (Square 3). This additional weight in the rear presses down on the cars suspension, affecting tire contact in the rear. If too much weight is applied, the rear tires spin.

Weight transfer to the front

Once more, the car is on our imaginary scales. The driver (Square 1) applies the brake (Square 6), shifting weight onto the front end of the car (Square 7). This time, the front-end weight increases and the rear-end weight decreases. In this case, if too much weight is shifted forward, the front tires will lock up and steering control will be lost.

Weight transfer to the left or right

With the car under way, the driver turns the steering wheel (Square 8). If the wheel is moved to the right, weight is transferred to the left once more, by way of the suspension and onto the tire contact patch.

Driving scenario — weight transfer in action

- You're driving your car, exiting a major highway, and entering the off ramp at a speed of 25 mph.

- Your car has tires with a 1,500-lb adhesion limit.

- By turning onto the off ramp, you have placed 1,400 lbs of force on your tires. This is fine, the tires can handle this unless, you have to apply the brakes or increase the angle of your turn. By doing either or both you will create more force on the tires, exceed their adhesion limits, and lose control of the car. Remember, if your vehicle has tires capable of accepting 1,500 lbs of vertical load, it can accept that load from braking, accelerating, or turning. It can take only 1,500 lbs.

If you use all 1,500 lbs accelerating, then try to turn or brake, you will reach the tires' adhesion limit and the tires will let go their grip on the pavement and you will lose control.

It is vital to understand the inter-relationships among acceleration, braking, and cornering (steering) forces. The ways in which they interact is one of the most important concepts in driving.

The amount you can move the steering wheel before losing adhesion is determined by how hard you have applied the brakes at the time. The opposite is also true; the amount of brakes you can apply is determined by how much steering force has been applied.

In later chapters we will discuss how to drive yourself out of trouble, concentrating on the fact that the foundation of trouble-free driving is the relationship between the forces of stopping, accelerating, and turning as represented by the brake and gas pedals and the steering wheel.

Chapter 15

YOU'RE REACTION TIME/ SENSE OF TIMING

What Is Reaction Time?

Many factors can affect your reaction time, but before we talk about them, let's find out just what reaction time is.

Reaction time is the sum of the time needed for:

1. The brain to receive information from the senses. The senses we're referring to also include sensations of motion and related "seat of the pants" sensations.

2. Making decisions on what to do next. Many times, this is a reflexive reaction that carries a potential for danger with it, such as immediately smashing down on the brake pedal when we feel the car begin to skid.

3. Transmission of the messages from the brain to the muscles needed to react and move the controls.

4. The muscles to respond.

The most critical portion of the reaction process is Step #2. After the senses detect the danger, a decision has to be made about what to do with the received information.

The challenges and dangers faced by racing drivers present a good example of this process.

Many racing drivers are surprisingly "old." Their reflexes may not be quite what they were when they were younger, but the decisions they make in the course of a race are the right ones.

These decisions are based on years of experience behind the wheel. Knowledge gained through experience often becomes intuitive and a part of our reflex reaction. Experienced pilots often gain this sort of reflexive knowledge.

	Reaction Time	Distance Traveled At 30 mph	Braking Distance	Total	
	0.6 sec 26.48 ft		45 ft	71.48 ft	
	0.8 sec 35.30 ft		45 ft	80.30 ft	
	1.0 sec 44.13 ft		45 ft	89.13 ft	
	1.5 sec 69.20 ft		45 ft	111.20 ft	
	2.0 sec 88.26 ft		45 ft	133.26 ft	

Reaction Time Diagram. The effects of various reaction times on total stopping distances.

A Hypothetical Example of Reaction Time — Sense of Timing

As an example, let's set up a hypothetical situation with two drivers, one young, and the other much older. Both are driving vehicles equipped with standard (non-ABS) brakes. (See Figure next page)

- They are both driving toward the same intersection from opposite directions.
- Ahead of them, a truck runs a stop sign and illegally enters the intersection so as to block the path of both drivers' cars.
- The younger driver gets his foot on the brake before the older driver, but smashes the pedal to the floor and locks up both wheels, enters an uncontrollable skid, and crashes into the truck.
- The older driver takes more time to react, but once he does, he brakes carefully, applies the proper amount of brake force and steering control and avoids the collision.
- The younger driver won the race to the brake pedal, but lost the battle with the truck.

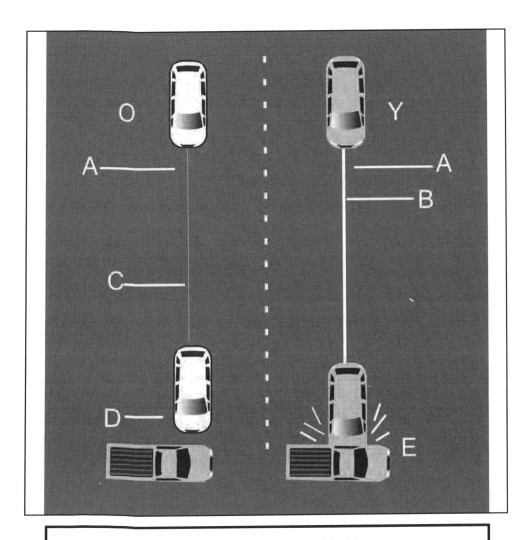

Reflexes vs Decision Making.

Car "Y" driven by young man.

Car "O" driven by older gentleman.

At point A both see emergency.

Car "Y" reaction time to get his foot to the brake is 0.5 SEC, which will use up 45 feet. Point B.

Car "O" reaction time to the brake is 1 SEC, which will use up 90 feet. Point C.

Car "Y" driver has slammed on the brake, locking up both wheels.

The car enters an uncontrollable skid, lasting 1.5 seconds or 135 feet.

Car "O" takes 0.5 SEC. To make a decision; he travels 45 feet.

- Without intuitive experience, the quickest decision can easily be the wrong decision.

Many Factors Other Than Age Affect Reaction Time

Reaction times can vary a great deal between people of the same age group.
Reaction times can vary according to the time of day — as much as four-tenths of a second in the morning to as much as a full second when a driver is fatigued at day's end. Four-tenths of a second may not sound like much, but at 60 mph a car travels 35 ft. in that amount of time. That could make a life and death difference in an accident situation. (See Figure)
Reaction times among tired or ill drivers can be as long as two full seconds. Again, at 60 mph, that means a driver will cover 123 ft. before reacting to a threat.

The standard reaction time for a healthy person is .75 sec., whereas reaction times among tired or ill drivers can be as long as two full seconds.

Decision Making Behind the Wheel

After an accident, some people might ask, **_Why did the driver just drive into the other car when there were so many other options open to him?_**

The answer could simply be that the driver could not reach a decision before it was too late. **The time required by the brain for a simple decision depends on how complex that decision is.**

- **A simple decision**, such as a reflex action, can be reached in three-tenths of a second.
- **If the problem faced by the brain is sufficiently complex** to require some thought, that decision can take as long as five-tenths to two full seconds, depending on the available options and the capabilities of the individual.

Over-Dependence on Reaction Time

The most important lesson to be learned about reaction time is that we know not to depend on it to get us out of trouble. The classic example of over-dependence on reaction time is encountered in the tailgater.

The Tailgater — The classic example of over dependence on reaction time.

We have all been plagued by this kind of driver – the one that drives too fast and so close you can practically count the fillings in his teeth in the rear-view mirror. An emergency can easily and quickly develop with no way for someone following you so closely to have adequate time and enough room to react. The tailgater is going to smash into you if you have to stop quickly, that's for sure.

If you were to pull that tailgater over and ask him why he follows you so closely, you might encounter someone who honestly doesn't know what you're talking about, someone that really doesn't consider what he's doing as dangerous or more disturbingly, someone who thinks he is Superman the super-driver that can react to anything, handle any driving emergency. Both attitudes are idiotic.

Training Can Improve Reaction Time

While it cannot make muscles move faster, good driver training can cut the time required in reaching a decision.

Through good training, a driver can experience situations simulating driving emergencies, which helps build the decision-making process.

Good training encourages the driver to focus attention on the proper course of action in a given emergency situation.

Good training helps drivers stay aware of their own limitations and that of their vehicles.

CHAPTER 16

TIRES

Tires, Part I Type and Quality

Tires, Part I

Type and Quality Make a Big Difference

Tires are one of the most important components of your car. The quality of control you maintain over your vehicle is only as good as the tires that vehicle rolls on. A car with outstanding handling qualities can have those qualities ruined by the installation of a poor set of tires.

So what do you need to know about the type and quality of the tires on your vehicle? Ideally, everything from the chemical compound of the rubber, to the tires construction (bias, bias-belted, or radial-ply), to the tread design (snow, all-weather, or conventional type passenger tires) and more. Depending on your particular driving situation, all these characteristics in combination would either add to, or detract from, the optimum handling qualities of your vehicle.

TIRE TREAD DESIGN

First of all, the purpose of tires is to create the road friction needed to do the things that can be done with cars, such as go, stop and turn. And the more rubber in contact with the road, the more traction you have up to a point. But your driving purpose and road conditions can dictate how much and what kind of traction is necessary. Many emergency vehicles, such as police cruisers, for example have tires wider than more conventional passenger cars for this reason. And, if we could guarantee that no rain or snow would ever fall, and that roads would

never get slippery, then we could use racing slicks (tires with no tread whatsoever) on all cars. (Racing tire rubbers include a compound that produces a maximum amount of friction with the road.) But if it rains, these tires are useless. All tire designs are compromises of some sort, surrendering one advantage in order to gain another.

All-Weather Tires

When the ground is covered with water, a good tire design swallows that water into the tread pattern and pushes it out to the sides of the tires. All-weather tires do this better than others. (Snow tires are completely different and require a different sort of design. See below.)

All-weather tires won't be as good as snow tires on some types of snow, and won't be better than performance tires in high-performance use, and may not last as long as a long-life passenger car tires but all-weather tires are still better than all the others in matching the broad variety of driving conditions encountered in everyday driving.

Snow tires offer deeper traction than standard.

Photo by Alekc79/Dreamstime

Snow Tires

Snow tires may enable you to deal better with snowy conditions, but the most important drawback to snow tires comes in the area of driving performance. They simply do not have the cornering performance of conventional tires. A car equipped with snow tires in the rear and conventional tires up front is much more likely to go out of control in emergency situations. Even worse, snow tires are not as good at stopping the car as conventional tires.

In snowy areas, many cities and counties have snow emergency regulations which are invoked during heavy snowfalls. Check with authorities for the rules in your area. Under some rules, motorists are subject to fines if they block traffic and do not have snow tires on their vehicles.

Chains offer greater traction than snow tires.

Photo © Lehman-Photo/Dreamstime

Chains and Studded Snow Tires

In areas where heavy snowfalls are frequent, many drivers carry chains for use in emergencies, or have their tire dealer apply studded snow tires for even greater traction.

Most states have time limits on use of studs, or ban them altogether. Before applying studded tires, check the regulations in your area.

If you use chains, make sure they are the proper size and type for your tires. Otherwise they may damage the tire sidewall and cause tire failure.

How to Decode a Tire

The Sidewall Story

The US Department of Transportation requires tire manufacturers to provide a wealth of information molded into the sidewall of every tire. Other useful information, not government mandated, may appear there as well.

The following examples will help you decode the tires already on your vehicle. Understanding the codes will help make you an informed tire purchaser and user, and will enable you to more easily follow the "latest" news in tire reports and testing.

Typical Information on the Sidewall of a Passenger Car Tire

A tire sidewall shows, for example, the name of the tire, its size, whether it is tubeless or tube type, the maximum load and maximum inflation, an important safety warning, and much more information.

The trouble is, most of this information is in code. For example, on the sidewall of a popular P-metric speed-rated auto tire, you'll find several codes:

Passenger Vehicle - Sidewall Outer Circle

P The "P" indicates the tire is for passenger vehicles.

Nominal Width
This three-digit number gives the width in millimeters of the tire from sidewall edge to sidewall edge. In general, the larger the number, the wider the tire.

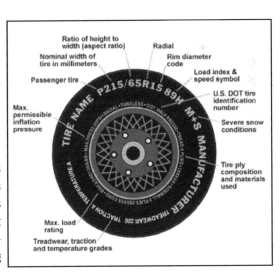

Aspect Ratio
This two-digit number, known as the aspect ratio, gives the tire's ratio of height to width. Numbers of 70 or lower indicate a short sidewall for improved steering response and better overall handling on dry pavement.

R The "R" stands for radial. Radial ply construction of tires has been the industry standard for the past 20 years.

Rim diameter code —This two-digit number is the wheel or rim diameter in inches. If you change your wheel size, you will have to purchase new tires to match the new wheel diameter.

Load index — This two- or three-digit number is the tire's load index. It is a measurement of how much weight each tire can support. You may find this information in your owner's manual. If not, contact a local tire dealer. Note: You may not find this information on all tires because it is not required by law.

Severe snow conditions — The "M+S" or "M/S" indicates that the tire has some mud and snow capability. Most radial tires have these markings; hence, they have some mud and snow capability.

Speed Rating — The speed rating denotes the speed at which a tire is designed to be driven for extended periods of time. The ratings range from 99 miles per hour (mph) to 186 mph. These ratings are listed below.

Q = 99 mph, H= 130 mph, R = 106 mph, V = 149 mph, S = 112 mph, W = 168 mph, T = 118 mph, Y = 186 mph U = 124 mph.

For tires with a maximum speed capability over 149 mph, tire manufacturers sometimes use the letters ZR. For those with a maximum speed capability over 186 mph, tire manufacturers always use the letters ZR.

You may not find this information on all tires because it is not required by law.

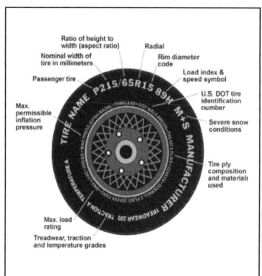

Sidewall Inner-Circle Codes

U.S. DOT Tire Identification Number begins with the letters "DOT" and indicates that the tire meets all federal standards. The next two numbers or letters are the plant code where it was manufactured, and the last four numbers represent the week and year the tire was built. For example, the numbers 3197 means the 31st week of 1997.

The other numbers are marketing codes, used to contact consumers if a tire defect requires a recall.

Tire Ply Composition and Materials Used

The number of plies indicates the number of layers of rubber-coated fabric in the tire. In general, the greater the number of plies, the more weight a tire can support. Tire manufacturers also must indicate the materials in the tire, which include steel, nylon, polyester, and others.

Maximum Load Rating

This number indicates the maximum load in kilograms and pounds that can be carried by the tire.

Maximum Permissible Inflation Pressure

This number is the greatest amount of air pressure that should *ever* be put in the tire under normal driving conditions.

Example Code: TREADWEAR 420

The DOT requires tire manufacturers to grade passenger car tires based on three performance factors: Treadwear, Traction, and Temperature Resistance.

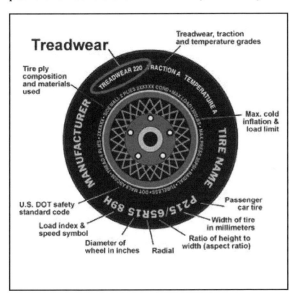

Tread-wear index or grade is a gauge of expected tread life, and is a comparative rating based on the wear rate of the tire when tested under controlled conditions on a specified government test track.

A tire graded 200 would wear twice as long on the government test course under specified test conditions as the "reference" one graded at 100.

A tread-wear rating of 420, means that (in theory, at least) the tire should last 4.2 times as long as the reference tire.

On typical tires, a tread-wear index of 180 is quite low, while an index of 500 is quite high. However, it is erroneous to link tread wear grades with your projected tire mileage. The relative performance of tires depends upon the actual conditions of their use, and may vary due to driving habits, type and condition of the vehicle, service practices, differences in road characteristics and climate.

Many observers within and without the tire industry have criticized the government-specified tests on several technical bases and because the tests are run by the tire makers themselves, without independent verification. The criticisms may be apt, but, as of now, the tread-wear index is the only game in town.

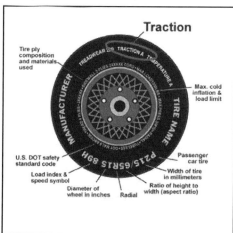

Example Code: TRACTION A

The traction grades, from highest (the best) to lowest (the worst), are A, B, and C. They represent the tires ability to stop on wet pavement as measured under controlled conditions on specified government test surfaces of asphalt and concrete.

The traction score is an index of straight-line stopping ability on a wet surface. Its an undemanding test. About half the passenger-car tires made are rated A.

Example Code: TEMPERATURE B

The temperature grade is an index of a tires ability to withstand the heat that high speeds, heavy loads, and hard driving generate.

The temperature grades are A (the highest), B and C, and represent the tires resistance to the generation of heat when tested under controlled conditions on a specified indoor laboratory test wheel.

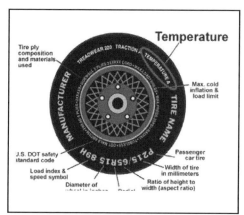

Temperature grades are an indication of a tire's resistance to heat. Sustained high temperature (driving long distances in hot weather), can deteriorate a tire to, leading to blowouts and tread separation. From highest to lowest, a tire's resistance to heat is graded as A, B, or C.

Typical Information on the Sidewall of a Light Truck Tire

LT - The "LT" indicates the tire is for light trucks.

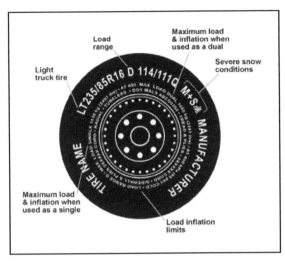

Max. Load Dual kg(lbs) at kPa(psi) Cold

This information indicates the maximum load and tire pressure when the tire is used as a dual, that is, when four tires are put on each rear axle (a total of six or more tires on the vehicle).

Max. Load Single kg(lbs) at kPa(psi) Cold indicates the maximum load and tire pressure when the tire is used as a single. **Load Range** identifies the tire's load-carrying capabilities and its inflation limits.

LT235/85R16 is the size designation for a metric light truck tire.

LOAD RANGED identifies the load and inflation limits.

RADIAL identifies that the tire has a radial construction.

MAX LOAD SINGLE 2623 lbs. AT 65 psi COLD indicates the maximum load rating of the tire and corresponding minimum cold inflation pressure for that load when used as a single.

MAX LOAD DUAL 2381 lbs. AT 65 psi COLD would indicate the maximum load rating of the tire and corresponding minimum cold inflation pressure when used in a dual configuration.

In simpler terms, when you have packed the maximum amount of weight allowed by the vehicle manufacturer, your inflation pressure should be whatever the recommendation marked on the tire suggests.

For normal operation, follow pressure recommendations in your owners manual or on the vehicle placard.

The other markings on the sidewall have the same meaning as described for the passenger car tire.

REPLACEMENT TIRE SELECTION

When tires need to be replaced, don't guess what tire is right for your vehicle. **Tire types are specific for each type of vehicle.**

As we'll see later under "Maintaining Traction," tires must be able to provide the friction necessary to handle the various maneuvers you put the vehicle through by accelerating, steering, and stopping all usually at speed. And when you do this, you're transferring a lot of different forces to each tire. The wrong tires on your vehicle could mean they simply won't be able to hold the road as they were designed to. And you'd probably find this out in a big hurry in an emergency situation.

To find out what type of tire you need for your vehicle, look at the **tire placard or sticker** that is attached to the vehicle on the door ledge, door post, or glove compartment. If your vehicle doesn't have a placard, check the owner's manual.

Tire Size and Construction

As you will see, that placard tells you the size and type of the tires which were on the vehicle as original equipment. Tires should always be replaced with the same size designation or approved options, as recommended by the automobile or tire manufacturer.

Never choose a smaller size with less load carrying capacity than the size on the tire placard.

Speed Rating

Some tires are now marked with letters to indicate their speed rating, based on laboratory tests which relate to performance on the road.

If the vehicle manual specifies speed-rated tires, the replacement tires must have the same or higher speed rating to maintain vehicle speed capability.

If tires with different speed ratings are mounted on the same vehicle, the tire or tires with the lowest rating will limit permissible tire-related vehicle speed.

> **When buying new tires, be sure your name, address and tire identification number (DOT code) are recorded and returned to the tire manufacturer or his record-keeping designee. Tire registration enables the manufacturer to notify you in the event of a recall.**

TIRE MOUNTING — DO'S AND DON'T'S

It is preferred that all four tires be of the same size, speed rating, and construction (radial or non-radial). But in some instances it may be necessary to use tires that do not match. Here are some guidelines:

- **Match tire size and construction designations in pairs on an axle** (or four tires in dual application), except for use of a temporary spare tire.
- If **two radial and two non-radial tires** are used on a vehicle, **put the radials on the rear.**

- If **two radial and two non-radial tires** are used on a vehicle equipped with dual rear tires, **the radials may be used on either axle.**

  Never mix radial and non-radial on the same axle except for use of a temporary spare tire.

- **Snow tires should be applied in pairs (or as duals) to the drive axle** (whether front or rear) or to all four positions.
- Never put **non-radial snow tires** on the rear if radials are on the front, except when the vehicle has duals on the rear.
- If **studded snow tires** are used on the front axle, studded tires also be used on the rear axle.
- Match all tire sizes and constructions on **four-wheel drive vehicles.**

  Only specially trained persons should demount or mount tires. An explosion of a tire and wheel assembly can result from improper or careless mounting procedures.

Tires − Part II
Care and Maintenance

Tires must be treated with care, for there are many factors that can affect their life and performance weather, driving habits, inflation pressure, vehicle alignment and wheel balance, and vehicle loading.

PROPER TIRE INFLATION PRESSURE

One of the most important maintenance procedures is checking your tires including the spare for proper inflation pressure.

With the right amount of air pressure, your tires wear longer, save fuel, and help prevent accidents. The right amount of air is the pressure specified by the vehicle manufacturer for the front and rear tires on your particular model car or light truck.

The Correct Air Pressure

The correct air pressure (cold tire pressure) is shown on the tire placard (or ticker) attached to the vehicle door edge, door post, or glove box door. If your vehicle doesn't have a placard, check the owners manual or consult with the vehicle or tire manufacturer for the proper inflation.

Inflation pressures are determined by the auto maker based on the cars weight and the anticipated load it will carry. However, it is difficult for the car builders to figure out exactly how much weight will be transferred to the front of the car during heavy braking. So, although a perfect tire pressure for all conditions is nearly impossible to come up with, the indicated psi is the one you should follow for most driving situations.

Care and Maintenance

Tires must be treated with care, for there are many factors that can affect their life and performance — weather, driving habits, inflation pressure, vehicle alignment and wheel balance, and vehicle loading.

PROPER TIRE INFLATION PRESSURE

One of the most important maintenance procedures is checking your tires **including the spare** — for proper inflation pressure.

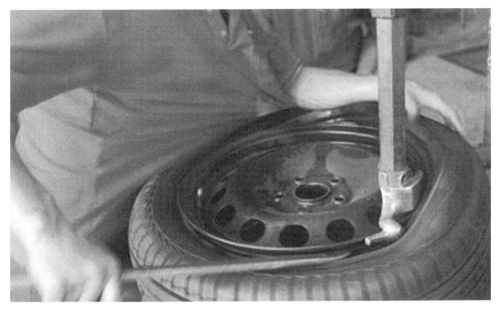
Tire mounting and unmounting is best done by a trained mechanic.
Photo © Dashark/Dreamstime

With the right amount of air pressure, your tires wear longer, save fuel, and help prevent accidents. The right amount of air is the pressure specified by the vehicle manufacturer for the front and rear tires on your particular model car or light truck.

> **REMEMBER: The tire pressure number that is molded into the sidewall of a tire is the tire maximum not the recommended inflation pressure.**

Freeway or expressway driving and tire inflation

Those who spend a lot of time in prolonged freeway or expressway driving (that is, routinely driving at a sustained speed of 60 mph) should increase tire pressure over the manufacturers recommended pressure as long as that pressure doesn't exceed the maximum psi figure printed on the tire sidewall.

4.0 psi increase in radial tires

5.5 psi increase in bias belted tires

7.0 psi increase in bias tires

Cold/hot weather driving and tire inflation

Many parts of the U.S. have cold weather driving conditions at least part of the year. Here are some things you should know about cold weather driving and its effects on tire inflation:

- **Every time the outside temperature drops 10 degrees Fahrenheit, the air pressure inside your tires goes down about one (1) pound per square inch.** You should check your tire pressures frequently during cold weather and add the necessary air to keep them at recommended levels of inflation at all times.
- Similarly, **pressure may increase when the temperature rises.**
- **Never reduce tire pressures in an attempt to increase traction on snow or ice.** It doesn't work and your tires will be so seriously under inflated that driving will damage them.

The new D-metric tires and tire inflation

If you are driving a car equipped with a set of the new D-metric tires (which will eventually replace the alpha-numeric size tires), you should know that **the D-metric tire pressures can be exceeded by two or three psi over the recommended pressures listed in the owners manual** or on the tire placard. Not only can these pressures be exceeded by a small amount, D-metric tires are inflated to a higher pressure overall.

Keeping Tires at Proper Pressure Is Easy

Its vitally important to keep track of the amount of air in your tires including the spare. Ideally, you should check the pressure:

- At least once a month
- When the temperature changes
- Before, during, and after every long trip

   Check your tires when they are COLD that is, when your vehicle has not been used for at least three hours.

Tire pressure gauges are inexpensive and fit in a pocket. There are many models to choose from. You can pick one up at most service stations and auto parts stores. Compressed air is available at almost every gas station.

   The hardest part to keeping tires properly inflated is simply taking the few moments required to do the job.

THE PERILS OF IMPROPER INFLATION

Under- or over inflation can cause tire failure/explosion of tire/rim assembly. In fact, most manufacturers now mold a safety warning on the sidewall that warns– serious injury may result from tire failure due to under inflation or overloading:

> **WARNING: Serious injury may result from tire failure due to under inflation/overloading. Follow owners manual or tire placard in vehicle.**

It is easier to go out of control on under inflated tires. **Tire pressure affects the tires ability to corner.** The sharper the turn required by a corner, the more effect tire pressure has. Sharp turn puts more stress on a tire than a gentle turn, and an under inflated tire accepts less stress before losing its grip on the pavement and going out of control. For example, a tire rated for inflation to 32 psi but only carrying 24 psi loses 10 percent of its handling capability on sharp turns.

A car is a weight-bearing machine. **Every time you move the controls, you are shifting weight throughout the vehicle.** These shifts are all eventually felt at the tires and the tires ability to bear that weight is dependent on the tire pressures.

Under inflation prematurely wears tires.

- The rule of thumb is that **a single pound of under inflation takes 500 miles off a tires life.** Most tires only last 70 percent of their design life, thanks to under inflation.
- **Tire pressures affect.** Properly inflated tires are part of the fuel economy equation. If a tire intended to be inflated to 32 psi is inflated to 24 psi, the result is a 20 percent boost in fuel consumption. This is because a properly inflated tire offers less rolling resistance than one that's under inflated, so it requires more energy to roll an under inflated tire than one with the proper amount of air in it, and in an automobile, energy is gasoline. If the tires on your car aren't properly inflated, you're wasting hundreds of miles worth of gasoline.

- **On the average, cars lose mileage at the rate of about a half a mile per gallon** if the tires fall six pounds below a recommended inflation of 25 pounds per square inch [psi].
- Under inflated tires also exhibit less overall durability and can be more easily damaged.
- **Tire type makes a difference.** Radial tires have two-thirds the rolling resistance of a cross- or bias-ply tire. Over 40,000 miles, a properly inflated radial tire pays for itself.

SYMPTOMS OF "SICK" TIRES

When tires get "sick," they show their drivers an abundant number of symptoms in plenty of time for the tires to be cured. By learning to read the early warning signs, you can prevent situations that both shorten tire life by thousands of miles, and that make those tires unsafe to drive on.

- When a tire is **under inflated**, most of its road contact is on the outer tread ribs, causing the outside edge of the tire to wear faster than the middle.
- With **over inflation**, the opposite wear appears. The center tread area bulges out slightly, causing it to wear faster than the outer ribs.

PROPER TIRE ROTATION

For maximum mileage and uniform tire wear, **rotate your tires every 5,000-6,000 miles**, and be sure to follow the correct rotation pattern for your vehicle as specified in your owner's manual

WORN TIRES

Worn tires are trouble. If you're driving on worn tires, you're driving without the tread depth that controls stopping, acceleration, and cornering. When driving on worn tires, you've thrown away some of the control you should have over your vehicle.

- Worn tires are **prone to hydroplaning,** are much **more susceptible to puncture** and could otherwise be hazardous.
- Studies showed that cars riding on tires with less than one-sixteenth of an inch of tread are up to 44 times more likely to blow-out.
- More than just unsafe, **worn tires are often illegal**. The Tire Industry Safety Council reports that 30 states now have laws on the books requiring that automobile tires have at least one-sixteenth of an inch of tread any less and the driver is issued a summons.

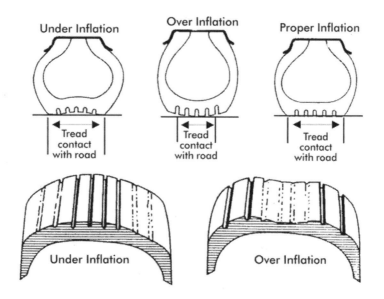

Under Inflation

Over Inflation

Proper Inflation

Tread contact with road

Tread contact with road

Tread contact with road

Under Inflation

Over Inflation

How Tires Look with Various Amounts of Inflation

TIRE ABUSE — YOURS AND NATURE'S

Wheel Spinning

Picture it: Your car is stuck in mud or in snow, or on a patch of ice.
If your first reaction is to shove the pedal to the metal and spin the tire free, you're only asking for more trouble, some of it quite serious.

A spinning tire creates friction, producing tremendous amounts of heat, and heat is a tire's worst enemy. This heat, combined with the centrifugal forces produced by spinning, could cause the tire to fail.

> **The worst case scenario for this situation is a catastrophic tire failure, resulting in tire detonation and the possibility of a dangerous shower of hot rubber!**

Most drivers don't realize just how fast their tires are spinning. A spinning tire's speed is often twice that displayed on the speedometer. To avoid problems, do not exceed 35 mph speedometer speed and make sure no one stands near the spinning tire.

As if all this tire danger weren't bad enough, **spinning the tires doesn't get the car free.** To free a trapped car, briefly rock the vehicle, tow it, or ap-

77

ply a traction aid such as sand or kitty litter to the surface under the tire. See "Getting Unstuck from Ice and Snow" Chapter.

Driving Speed

The faster you drive, the faster you'll wear out your tires. As a car is driven, the rear wheels press down on the pavement. At 30 mph, the rear tires exert a 5 horse power (hp) push against the pavement.

At 50 mph 15 hp are exerted, and by 70 mph, this figure grows to 38 hp.

Temperature and Temperature Changes

Temperature also has an extreme effect on tires. Low temperatures, or changes in temperature wear tires out faster.

The distance between the rim of a US penny and Lincoln's head is 1/16 of an inch – the minimum safe tread depth.

Photo © Joyce Huber

Tests have shown that a change from a winter temperature such as 41 degrees fahrenheit to a hot summer day temperature of 95 degrees Fahrenheit increases tire wear 400 percent, all other conditions being equal.

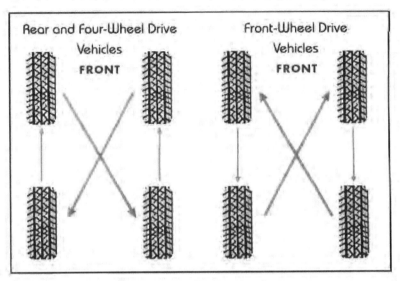

Common Correct Tire Rotation Patterns.
Image courtesy NHTSA

CHAPTER 17

Winter Driving

Changes in the weather conditions can challenge the most experienced driver. Before setting out, clean your windshield, back window and side mirrors.

When driving from dry road conditions onto icy roads, the **traction to maneuver your vehicle decreases by 65%**. Driving from snow to ice decreases the vehicles maneuvering capability by 49%.

Even four-wheel-drive (4-WD) systems do not alter the 65% decrease in traction. If there is less adhesion between tire and road, the vehicles capability is greatly diminished.

Four-wheel-drive equipped vehicles, however, are useful in bad weather to maneuver up snow covered hills and to get the vehicle moving from a stop position when two-wheel drive (2-WD) cannot.

The problem is that some 4WD/AWD (all wheel drive) drivers mistakenly believe their vehicle can defy the laws of physics. However, **once the vehicle is moving the laws of physics for all vehicles are equal.**
A 4WD vehicle will do a better job of getting the vehicle moving than a 2WD vehicle. But, once the brakes are applied, a 4WD is like all other vehicles, the driver is at the mercy of the tire to road adhesion.

• On a steep hill with packed snow, **4WD is a big help**, but driving up the same hill on ice it's of very little help.

• Only **chains** increase traction of rubber tires on snow and ice significantly.

• **Stopping** on snow and ice may require up to 10 times the distance as stopping in normal conditions.

• When driving in bad weather **the best advice is slow down.**

An all too familiar scene for those living in northern climates. Photo © Photka/Dreamstime

Extreme Cold Weather

The best protection against the cold is to keep the car out of the elements. If you can't keep the car out of the elements, turn off all the accessories, the radio, heater, and wipers, so it won't have to work as hard to start. **The most common problem in extreme cold is having a battery too weak to start the engine.**

When purchasing a battery check **the cold-cranking amp rating,** the higher the number the better your car will start in cold weather.

For real extreme cold you can install **an engine block heater** to keep the engine block warm. When traveling through some of the northern states in winter, you'll find inns and hotels that have electrical outlets at parking spaces, so you can plug in the heater while the car is turned off.

Antifreeze

Antifreeze can go bad. New and undiluted antifreeze can handle temperature as low as 40° F below, But if your antifreeze is rated for five below, and it's going to be 15° below, your car won't be protected. Before temperatures drop, have your dealer or local garage check the temperature rating of your antifreeze. You can buy antifreeze testers at the local auto store.

An antifreeze tester is used to determine the freeze point of the antifreeze.
Photo © Jack Schiffer/Dreamstime

Windshield Washer Fluid

Keep the reservoir of your wiper fluid filled up. You can also cover the windshield and keep the snow or ice away from the wipers.

CHAPTER 18
Getting Unstuck from Snow and Ice

Many times snow will build up in front of the wheels acting as a barrier to the vehicle getting unstuck. **Carry a shovel in your vehicle and clear the snow from around all the tires.** It makes an enormous difference.

If you're still stuck, you'll need to put something between the tires and the snow that will create traction. **Try spreading some sand or kitty litter around the tires.** In fact, it is a good idea to carry some cat litter in your trunk along with the shovel. If you can't find sand or litter, try anything that might create traction. Place whatever you are using under the drive wheels — the front wheels for a front-wheel drive car and the back wheels for a rear-wheel drive car. Auto supply stores sell special mats and traction devices just for this occasion, but **in an emergency, you can use your floor mats for traction.**

Create some momentum to get the vehicle moving. If you have an automatic

Pushers should not stand directly behind the wheels to avoid being hit by flying gravel, floor mats, sand or ice.   Photo © Sergey Lavrentev/dreamstime_

transmission, **put the vehicle in low gear,** for is a manual transmission into second gear and gently apply pressure to the accelerator. **If the wheels start spinning, ease off gas pedal.**

If the above is not working, **try slowly rocking the car.** Move forward, when the car will no longer go forward, release the accelerator and allow the car to roll back.

When the vehicle stops its backward motion, apply minimum pressure to the gas pedal accelerator again. Repeat the rocking action in rapid succession until the vehicle rolls free. **Don't do this for extended period of time – it can raise hell with the automatic transmission or clutch.** If there are people available they can assist the car's rocking motion, by pushing.

Snow chains are attached to the drive wheels of a vehicle. This photo shows a woman putting chains on a front-wheel drive car.

Chains are sold in pairs and must match the tire diameter and tread width. Driving with chains will reduce fuel efficiency and slow down the speed of the automobile. Photo © monkeybusinessimages/dreamstime

> **Those who are pushing the vehicle should not stand directly behind the wheels because of the risk from flying gravel, floor mats, sand and ice.**

The pusher need to be aware of his own footing too. Ice can be hazardous. If you use pushers, **create signals between the people** doing the pushing and the driver. This will go a long way to avoid an accident. You don't want to run over the people who are helping you.

If the vehicle is still stuck and you decide to wait for help, **set up reflectors or flares visible to passing motorists.**

If you opt to stay with the car, **do something that will let people know**

you are in the car and need help. Auto stores have an array of products that fit that need. If you run the heater it is imperative that you insure that the exhaust pipe is not blocked with snow and leave the windows cracked.

Keep a cell phone with you and think about investing in **On Star.** In scenarios like this, it can be a life saver.

When you're stuck, a cell phone can be a life saver

Photo © Richard Nelson/dreamstime

CHAPTER 19
Night Driving Tips

Most drivers think the only difference between day and night driving is the need for headlights. True, but headlights are a poor substitute for daylight.

Even during daylight, safe driving depends not only on as far as you can see, but on how much you can see, and how fast you can see it and react to it. After the sundown, all these factors change dramatically.

- **Keep your headlights in good working order**. Make sure your headlights are aligned properly.
- **Keep headlights clean,** especially in the winter. As much as half of headlights total illumination can be absorbed by dirt on the surface of the glass beam.
- **Keep your eyes moving**, don't just focus on the middle of the lighted area in front of you.
- **When backing up**, remember that only your backup lights are available; on most makes of cars, they aren't much.
- If the high beams of an oncoming car are not dimmed, **avoid looking directly at the bright lights**. Glance toward the right side of the road; then quickly look ahead to determine the other vehicles position.
- **Take breaks when driving long distances**. Continual glare of lights outside and from your dashboard increase the chance of highway hypnosis.
- **Use low beams when following a vehicle**.
- **Use high-beams when it is safe and legal.** Switch to low beams if following another car or encountering on-coming cars to avoid blinding the other driver.

If you have to pull off the road:

- Turn on your vehicle's **emergency flashers**.
- Turn on the cars **interior or dome lights.**

If the cars electrical system fails, have a combination of flares, a flashlight, and some reflective materials handy.

Driving Past Bedtime

 A person's alertness level decreases around the time one routinely retires for the night. If you must drive past your usual bedtime:
• Stop every hour or so and walk around.
• Stretch your legs.
• Get some air.

CHAPTER 20

DISTRACTED DRIVING

What Is Distracted Driving?

There are three main types of distraction:

- Visual — taking your eyes off the road.
- Manual — taking your hands off the wheel.
- Cognitive — taking your mind off what you're doing.

Distracted driving is any non-driving activity a person engages in that has the potential to distract him or her from the primary task of driving and increase the risk of crashing.

While all distractions can endanger drivers' safety, **texting is the most alarming because it involves all three types of distraction.**

Other distracting activities include:

- Using a cell phone.
- Eating and drinking.
- Talking to passengers.
- Grooming.
- Reading, including maps.
- Using a PDA or navigation system.
- Watching a video.
- Changing the radio station, CD or Mp3 player.

Pull off the road if you must make a call. Photo © Glen Jones/dreamstime

Did You Know?

Research collected by the National Highway Traffic Safety Administration. on distracted driving reveals some surprising facts:

- 20% of injury crashes in 2009 involved reports of distracted driving. (NHTSA).
- In 2009, 5,474 people were killed in U.S. roadways and an estimated additional 448,000 were injured in motor vehicle crashes that were reported to have involved distracted driving. (FARS* and GES*).

Fatality Analysis Reporting System (FARS), which became operational in 1975, contains data on a census of fatal traffic crashes within the 50 states, the District of Columbia, and Puerto Rico. Data for GES come from a nationally representative sample of police reported motor vehicle crashes of all types, from minor to fatal.

- The age group with the **greatest proportion of distracted drivers was the under-20 age group** – 16 % of all drivers younger than 20 involved in fatal crashes were reported to have been distracted while driving. (NHTSA)
- Drivers who use hand-held devices **are four times as likely to get into crashes serious enough to injure themselves.** (Source: Insurance Institute for Highway Safety)

Examination of Driver Distraction

Driver distraction could present a serious and potentially deadly danger. In 2009, an estimated 448,000 people were injured in motor vehicle crashes that were reported to have involved distracted driving. **Distracted driving comes in various forms, such as cell phone use, texting while driving, eating, drinking, talking with passengers, as well as using in-vehicle technologies and portable electronic devices.**

There are other less obvious forms of distractions including **daydreaming or dealing with strong emotions.**

While these numbers are significant, they may not state the true size of the problem, since the identification of distraction and its role in a crash can be very difficult to determine using only police-reported data. New data sources are available to provide more details on the type and presence of driver distraction.

Fatalities

- In 2009, there were 30,797 fatal crashes in the United States, which involved 45,230 drivers. In those crashes 33,808 people died.

- In 2009, 5,474 people were killed in crashes involving driver distraction (16% of total fatalities).

- The proportion of fatalities reportedly associated with driver distraction increased from 10% in 2005 to 16% in 2009. Fatal crashes with reported driver distraction increased from 10% to 16%.

- The portion of drivers reportedly distracted at the time of the fatal crashes increased from 7% in 2005 to 11% in 2009.

- The **under-20 age group had the highest proportion of distracted drivers involved in fatal crashes** (16%). The age

Using a cell phone while driving, whether it's hand-held or hands-free, delays a driver's reactions as much as having a blood alcohol concentration at the legal limit of .08 percent. (Source: University of Utah)   Photo © Joyce Huber

group with the next greatest proportion of distracted drivers was the 20- to-29-year-old age group. Thirteen percent of all 20-to-29-year-old drivers in fatal crashes were reported to have been distracted.

- Of those drivers reportedly distracted during a fatal crash, **the 30-to-39-year-old drivers were the group with the greatest proportion distracted by cell phones.** Cell phone distraction was reported for 24 % of the 30-to-39-year-old distracted drivers in fatal crashes.

- **Light-truck drivers and motorcyclists** had the greatest percentage of total drivers reported as distracted at the time of the fatal crash (12% each). Bus drivers had the lowest percentage (6%) of total drivers involved in fatal crashes that were reported as distraction-related.

- An estimated **20% of 1,517,000 injury crashes were reported to have involved distracted driving in 2009.**

It's illegal to use a cell phone while driving in several states. You run the risk of a hefty ticket in some areas. If you must use your cell phone, pull off the road.

State laws for cell phone use as of 1/2011

Alabama: Cell and texting Illegal for novice drivers 16 or 17 with intermediate or <6 Mo.s primary.

Alaska: Texting is Illegal for all drivers with the enforcement being primary.

Arizona: Bans school bus drivers from cell use.

Arkansas: Bans all from cell and texting use.

California: Bans drivers from cell and texting use.

Colorado: Bans <18, all from texting.

Connecticut: Illegal for all drivers.

Delaware: Bans drivers from cell and texting use.

D.C.: Bans all drivers from cell and texting use.

Florida: No laws.

Georgia: Bans school bus drivers from cell phone use; all drivers from texting.

Hawaii: No state laws, but all counties have distracted driving ordinances.

Idaho: No use Laws, lists distractions in/on vehicle if there is an accident.

Illinois: Bans school bus drivers and under 19 from cell phone, bans all texting.

Indiana: Bans those under 18 from talking or texting.

Iowa: Bans restricted or intermediate license from cell, all from texting.

Kansas: Only bans those with a learners license from talking; Bans all texting.

Kentucky: Bans school bus drivers from cell phone use; bans all texting.

Louisiana: Bans learner or intermediate license, school bus drivers and 1st year of license from cell use; bans all texting.

Maine: Only bans those under 18 from hand-held cell use; bans all texting.

Maryland: Bans handheld talking; bans all use for under 18; bans all texting.

Massachusetts: Bans school bus drivers, under 18 from all cell phone use; bans all texting.

Michigan: Bans all texting; bans teens with probationary licenses from all cell phone use.

Minnesota: Bans all cell phone and texting.

Mississippi: Bans school bus drivers from all use; bans learner or provisional from texting.

Missouri: Bans drivers under 21 from texting.

Montana: No laws.

Nebraska: Bans those under 18 from cell phone use; bans all texting.

Nevada: No laws.

New Hampshire: Bans all texting.

New Jersey: Bans all hand held cell use, bans learners and school bus drivers from all cell use. Bans all texting.

New Mexico: Bans handheld in state vehicles; bans learners from all cell use and texting.

New York: Bans hand held cell use and texting.

North Carolina: Bans school bus drivers and those under 18 from all cell use; bans texting.

North Dakota: Bans under 18 from cell use, bans all texting.

Ohio: No laws.

Oklahoma: Bans learners and intermediate licensed drivers from hand held cell phones and texting, bans schoolbus drivers from all cell phone use and texting.

Oregon: Bans all hand held cell, bans under 18 from all cell phones, bans all texting.

Pennsylvania:

Rhode Island: Only illegal for school bus drivers and those under 18 to talk on cell phones while driving. Bans all from texting.

South Carolina: , Has distracted attributes under Contributing Factors for accidents.

South Dakota: No laws.

Tennessee: Only illegal for school bus drivers and those under 18 to talk on cell phones while driving. Bans all texting.

Texas: Bans all from texting. Bans school bus drivers and those under 18 to talk on cell phones while driving.

Utah: Defines careless driving as a moving violation if driving while distracted.

Vermont: Illegal for school bus drivers and under 18 from cell phones. Bans all from texting.

Virginia: Bans under 18 and school bus drivers from cell phone use. Bans all from texting.

Washington: Illegal for all drivers to use handheld cell phones. <18 bans all use. Bans texting.

West Virginia: Illegal for those with a learner's license or under 18 to talk or text on cell phones.

Wisconsin: Bans all from texting.

Wyoming: Bans all from texting.

Sources: Insurance Institute for Highway Safety (IIHS) and State Highway Safety Offices.

Disclaimer: Information is for general information purposes only. For clarification on any law consult the appropriate State Highway Safety Office.

CHAPTER 21

ROAD RAGE

How to Avoid It, How to Deal with It

Not like there isn't enough to worry about when we are driving, we now have to cope with another potentially deadly problem, road rage.

Anyone who drives on the road these days knows the problem. As you are driving, someone makes an obscene gesture at you, calls you names that are not flattering, questions your parenthood. He may even start tailgating you for long distances, or deliberately cutting you off, or trying to force you off the road. His emotions have gotten the best of him, his anger has boiled over, and he's turned downright aggressive and ready to risk your life and his. And for what?

What Starts Road Rage?

The American Automobile Association (AAA) indicates that road rage is often started over trivial things you honked your horn too much, or at all; you took (or wanted to take) a parking space someone else had their eye on. Or maybe you committed the "mortal sin" of slowing someone down, or inadvertently did something that wasn't in the best interest of automotive safety — cut someone off, zigzagged in and out of traffic, or tailgated because you were in a hurry or just not paying attention.

On the other hand, maybe the other driver got behind the wheel already enraged by something, and you were just unlucky enough to be on the same road with her at the same time.

Whatever the reason, road rage situations can escalate to collisions, disputes and even death.

Who Commits Road Rage?

If you decide to engage a "road rager" in conversation or worse, decide to play road warrior with him please understand whom you may be dealing with.

According to the American Automobile Association, "road ragers" are mostly poorly educated males between the ages of 18 to 26 with criminal records. They have histories of violence, drug abuse, or alcohol problems, and many have suffered an emotional or professional setback.

Many impatient drivers set themselves up to be victims of road rage. They take risks on the road, which can lead to discourteous driving, which can lead to disputes, which can es-calate into road rage.

You may become enraged yourself "sick and tired" of dealing with aggressive drivers who are "jerks," "idiots," "who

Impatient drivers take risks, which can lead to road rage. Don't take traffic problems personally.
Photo © Joyce Huber

don't have all their wagons in a circle," "who have the intelligence quotient of a Styrofoam cup." They can all get you heated up and make you lose your pa-tience, make you do things and take risks you normally wouldn't. They can drag you into their road rage game if you let them. Don't. It can be a deadly game.

Things to Do/Don't Do to Avoid or Deal with Road Rage

The general rule is to avoid all conflicts. If another driver wants to get by, let him pass. If she wants a parking space, let her have it. Consider it a contribu-tion to you favorite charity. **If another driver challenges you, don't chal-lenge back. Let him go.**

Here are some suggestions from the AAA and then some on how to avoid and deal with road rage.

- **DON'T take traffic problems personally.** Believe it or not, traffic is not an organized conspiracy to prevent you from being on time.
- **DO give yourself enough time** to get where you are going.
- **DON'T automatically assume other drivers mistakes are purposely aimed at you.**

- **If a driver has done something stupid to you** or simply made a mistake, **DON'T return the favor.** In other words, don't have a contest to see who is the dumbest, you may just win.
- **AVOID eye contact with aggressive drivers;** it only encourages them.

- **If an aggressive driver makes an obscene gesture, DON'T make one or two back at him**. Although it may be incredibly gratifying, it brings you to his level and can escalate the situation.
- **If an aggressive driver pursues you,** Do find the nearest police station.
- **BE CAREFUL about using your horn** as a method of communicating **even a friendly honk can be misinterpreted.**
- **DON'T** honk excessively.
- **DON'T** use high-beam headlights unnecessarily.
- If you drive slowly, DO pull over and let people pass you.
- **DON'T block the passing lane.** No matter how fast you are going, there will always be someone who wants to go faster.
- **DON'T** switch lanes without signaling first.
- **AVOID** blocking the right hand turn lane.
- **DON'T** tailgate.
- **DON'T** take up more than one parking place.
- **DON'T** allow your door to hit the car next to you when exiting your car in a parking lot.
- **DON'T** inflict your loud music on nearby cars.
- **REMEMBER:** Always be polite and courteous on the road, even if another driver is acting like an idiot.

CHAPTER 22

PERSONAL SAFETY*

Alone Behind the Wheel

Two violent crimes are committed in the U.S. every minute of every day. Drivers traveling alone can be particularly vulnerable. There are a number of things you can do, however, to keep yourself safe. Both inside your car and out. Read about those things here, then pass the information along to anyone who might be alone behind the wheel.

What should I know about parking safety?

Lots. Where and how you choose to park can go a long way toward keeping you safer.

- When possible, **back into a parking space**. Should you need to, you'll be able to drive out with less chance of someone trapping you.

- Try to **park close to the building entrance**. This will reduce the time You're alone outside your car.

- If you know you're going to be working late, **move your car to a well-lighted area closer to the exit**. Such a precaution may reduce your risk at night.

- If you're in a parking lot, always **choose a spot that will be well-lighted and away from shrubs and bushes** so you can see under and around your car as you approach it.

Should I do anything special in parking garages?

- Yes. Park in a well-lighted spot, ground level if available, close to the parking attendant station.

- If you can't do that, try to **park close to the elevators or stairwell near the building entrance.**

- **Spend as little time as possible** going to and from your car.

Note: Sections of this chapter are courtesy of Shell Oil

- Try to **stay where you can be seen by others** because there's safety in numbers.
- If you have any concerns at all, call the buildings security service and **have someone accompany you to your car**.

If I lock my car before I leave it, is that enough?
- No. You should take additional precautions.
- If you have a two-door car, **flip your passenger seat forward** when You're leaving your vehicle.
- If its a four-door car, **move the driver seat forward**.

Upon your return, if you see that it has been returned to its original position, go back to the building you came from immediately and notify security of the police. **Someone could be hiding on the back floorboard.**

As you approach your car, don't just look around it; look under it as well. Criminals sometimes hide there.

I hear a lot about car jackings. Is there any way to avoid them?

The FBI estimates that approximately 25,000 car jackings occur in the U.S. each year. There are defensive techniques you can use that might keep you from becoming a carjacking victim.

- Always **keep your doors locked**.
- Always **scan ahead and behind as you drive**. Look for individuals who may be loitering near an intersection.
- If it looks as if you may be driving into a potentially dangerous situation at an upcoming intersection, slow down and, if you can do so safely, **time the light to avoid stopping**. Be sure there is no cross traffic that could cause a collision.

Try to **keep escape routes open**. Stop far enough behind the car in front of you so that you can see its back tires touching the pavement. That way, if you have to pull out quickly, you won't have to back up first. Also, stay in the left-hand lane when approaching an intersection.

What's that bump and run carjacking thing?

Its a technique carjackers often employ. People in one car pull up behind an unsuspecting driver and bump that drivers car. When the driver gets out to inspect the damage, the carjackers forcibly take control of the car and the driver. If you believe that you've been intentionally bumped, don't stop and get out of the car. Drive to a safe, public place close by to check the damage. You'll be a lot less vulnerable.

Got any safety trip tips?

- DO **plan your trip before you leave**. Mark your route (how you're going and where you plan to stop) on a map. Give a copy of that plan (with appropriate phone numbers where you can be reached and an estimated time of arrival) to a family member, friend, or business associate.

- DON'T take maps or other obvious travel aids into rest stops or restaurants. **You don't want to call attention to the fact that you have a long way to travel**.
- DO **check your car out completely before you get on the road**. Many breakdowns are avoidable, especially those involving fuel, oil, cooling or electrical problems.
- DON'T think just because you have a cellular phone that you won't need to use a public one. Carry a prepaid phone card, just in case.
- DO **use valet parking at hotels and restaurants**. Its safer than spending too much time in the parking lots. But, make sure the restaurant has valet parking. One woman gave her new Mercedes' keys to a smiling man in a blue uniform who was standing outside a restaurant door. She later found out that restaurant did not offer valet parking.
- **DON'T try to fix a flat if you think you are in an unsafe area**. Drive slowly to a service station or police station.

Should I always have my door locked when I'm driving?

Yes. All your doors. And, you should always have your windows rolled up. If its hot and you don't have air conditioning, roll your windows down just enough to allow air to flow in, but not enough to allow someone to get his hand in the car.

What do I do if my car just conks out?

- If your car comes to a stop slowly, try to **pull safely off the road**, out of the way of traffic.
- **Stay in your car**.
- If you have a cell phone, **call for help and give them your location**. If you don't have roadside assistance service, call the police.
- If you don't have a cell phone, **stick a white handkerchief or scarf part way out your window.** This will alert passers-by that you need assistance.

- If someone does stop to help you, stay inside your car with all the doors locked and the windows rolled up high enough so no one can get a hand inside the car. Tell them what kind of help you need. If their concern is genuine, they'll make a call for you or alert someone who can help you at their next stop.
- Don't get out and raise the hood of your car. This blocks your view of oncoming traffic (one of whom may be a policeman), and it signals the potential criminal that your car is immobile.
- You should **always carry a Call Police window sign** in your glove compartment (or have paper and marker to make one). That way many drivers will see that you need help, and if someone does stop that you are suspicious of, you can tell him that someone saw your sign and has already contacted the police, who are currently en route.

Is Having a phone in the car a good idea?

Yes. But it can be dangerous if not used properly. **People using a phone while driving run a 34% higher risk of having a collision**.
NOTE: Several cities and areas have adopted a no cell phone use while driving ordinance.

- **If you must dial, pull safely off the road,** stop, then dial. Headset or speaker phone units that allow you to talk and listen without holding a receiver are better, but they can still be dangerous if they pull your attention away from the road.
- If you **preprogram your phone to activate 9-1-1** or other emergency numbers, you'll be able to react more quickly in an emergency.
- It's best to **use the phone in the car only as an emergency aid** or to let people at your destination know in advance if you are going to be late. That's better than trying to drive too fast to get there on time.

I seem to get more tired when I drive alone. What can I do about it?
Driver fatigue can be a killer. It's especially dangerous when you are alone. Here are some things you can do to help stay awake:

- **Begin your trip early in the day.** Get plenty of sleep before you drive.
- **Avoid long drives at night.** The glare of lights outside and from your dashboard increases the chance of highway hypnosis.
- **Adjust your car's environment to help you stay awake.** Keep the temperature cool. Don't use cruise control. Keep your body involved in the drive.
- **Use good posture.** Keep your head up, shoulders back, buttocks tucked against the seat back, legs not fully extended.
- **Take frequent breaks.** Stop at well-lighted rest areas or service stations, and get out of the car to stretch or have a snack.
- **Avoid alcohol** entirely.
- Don't allow your eyes to become fatigued. **Wear sunglasses to fight glare during the day.**
- **Break the monotony.** Vary your speed levels. Chew gum. Talk to yourself. Listen to talk radio.

If you absolutely cannot keep your eyes open, **the best remedy is to stop and get some sleep**. Staying at a motel for the night is usually the safest bet. If you cannot find a motel, it is still better to be off the road than to fall asleep while driving. If you do pull off the road to take a quick nap, be sure you are safely off the road, preferably at a well-lighted, secure rest area, service plaza or truck stop, with all doors locked. If a security guard is present, ask him or her to keep an eye on your car while you're napping.

What if I plan and prepare but someone confronts me anyway?

Your foremost concern should be your personal safety. If you are confronted by a robber or a carjacker, don't resist. Give up your purse, your wallet and your keys quickly. Do not attempt to reason with a robber. Try to remember what the individual looks like.

Remember, possessions can be replaced. Your life can't be.

Chapter 23
The Driving System and Accident Causes

The Driving System

Your ability to avoid accidents does not depend solely on your ability to control the car. When driving a car, you're at the mercy of the environment around you and at the mercy of the vehicle you are driving.

Like Mother Nature, driving is a balance, and that balance is called the "driving system." The driving system is made up of three components: THE DRIVER, THE MACHINE, and THE ENVIRONMENT. When an automotive accident occurs, it is caused by a failure of the driving system. Either the driver, the vehicle, or the environment failed.

The Driver

The driver is the only truly flexible, adaptable factor of the driving system triangle. The driver is responsible for the successful implementation of the DRIVER/ MACHINE relationship. If the driving system fails, only the driver suffers.

The proof lies in the numbers. Some 89 percent of all vehicular accidents are caused by driver error (this number is clouded by the fact that 48 percent of that 89 percent figure is directly attributable to accidents caused by drinking). But the remaining 41 percent were clear-headed drivers who got into trouble.

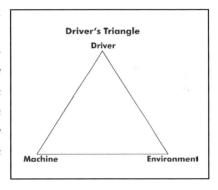

The Machine

A little-known fact about cars is that most of them are good handling vehicles. However, no matter how well a vehicle handles, it is only a machine, and like all machines, has its limitations. These limitations are aggravated when maintenance is poor or insufficient, but accidents caused by outright mechanical failure are relatively rare. Accidents due to impaired vehicle performance due to poor or relaxed maintenance standards are difficult, if not impossible, to compute.

Text messaging, cell phone use, grooming and other distractions that take your hands off the wheel and/or your eyes off the road can lead to fatal accidents. In fact, simply edging out of your lane for a couple of seconds can cause a disaster.   Photo © Picsfive/Dreamstime

The Environment

The United States has the best-designed and constructed highway system in the world. Nevertheless, these roads are not immune to the effects of weather and use. If the road surface has been modified by nature, then the driver and machine portion of the driving system must cope with these changes.

In some rare instances the road conditions have deteriorated to the point that the driver/machine combination cannot compensate.

It is the environmental portion of the driving system that puts drivers at a distinct disadvantage. People drive in all sorts of weather conditions, when they do they are at the mercy of the environment.

The Driving Problem
Auto accidents are the fourth leading cause of death in the U.S. This figure gives us an idea of the size of the problem we are dealing with here. The biggest problem with driving is driver error. From the numbers alone, it's obvious we're doing something wrong.

Yet, most people find it difficult to recognize their driving deficiencies. In fact, you'd be hard-pressed to find anyone who realizes there's more to learn than merging onto highways and parallel parking. Most US driver's earned their license by attending a high school, driver-education program, and then were tested by the local authorities for proficiency in parking and awareness of rules of the road. After passing our written and road tests and receiving our license to drive, we assumed we had become instant experts.

The simple fact is that **we don't become competent drivers until we get some driving experience under our belt.** We become good or bad drivers through the types of driving experiences we have had. If we manage to survive these experiences, there is usually no problem.

Legends get Caution

The old "there's an infamous intersection near here where all the accidents happen" story. It's an experience all drivers go through. We all have one intersection nearby that's known far and wide as a dangerous place to drive; the sort of intersection you're plain lucky to survive. You probably have to drive through that intersection on your way to school or work, and when you do cross it, you do so with caution. Why? Because experience and local legend have taught you that this intersection is dangerous and deserves caution.

Accidents are Not Always Accidental

They are an unexpected events that happen by chance and are caused by breakdowns in the driving system. Through research, it is possible to determine the cause of an accident, learn from it and gain skills to avoid it. **Surprisingly, most accidents are caused by driver error.**

Plus, some drivers are extremely unwilling to do this. People disassociate themselves from accidents. At the *Tony Scotti Vehicle Dynamics School*, I find hundreds of drivers, who were involved in accidents, talk about them as though they weren't anywhere near the car when it crashed.

Consider the person who says, "My car was hit by another car that went through a stop sign." To listen to this person, you'd think that no one was in either car at the time of the accident! **Cars don't drive past stop signs all by themselves.** Once we accept the fact that we can actually get ourselves into an accident, and that in most cases it will either be you or the other driver who is the cause of the accident, then the next important concept to understand is the type of accident we are likely to become involved in.

JUST HOW DO ACCIDENTS HAPPEN?

If we know the types of driving conditions that produce the greatest number of accidents, then we can be more alert during these conditions.

Two-car collisions

Ninety-six percent of all two-car collisions (excepting two-car fatal collisions) can be described as taking place under three separate conditions:

- **The most frequent type of two-car collision is the side collision.** Out of all two-car collisions, 44.6 percent are side collisions. The most common type of two-car crash occurs when both cars are traveling in parallel courses and one crosses the path and hits the side of the other.

- **The second most frequent type of accident is the rear-end collision.** Some 27.7 percent of the accidents discussed here fall into this category. This usually happens when one vehicle is stopped and the second car, overtaking from the rear in a straight line, hits the stopped car.

- **The second most common rear-end crash involves the striking vehicle hitting a parked car.**

- The third most common two-car accident type is a bit unusual. Amounting to 13.6 percent of the two-car, non-fatal accidents, **this is the kind of head-on collision in which the two vehicles are not traveling straight toward each other.** In this category, the most common accident scenario involves a striking vehicle making a left-hand turn and impacting a car coming the other way head on.

- **The second most frequent type of head-on crash does involve both cars traveling in straight lines, directly at each other.**

Rear-end collisions are the second most common.
Photo © Pavel Vorobyev, Dreamstime

Single-car accidents

The statistics for single-car accidents are very different than those for two-car collisions. According to the figures, **in some 50 percent of all single-car accident, the car was out of control before it hit anything or went off the road.** This means that something happened to cause the driver to lose control. **Amazingly, in 40 percent of the single-car mishaps, the car was traveling in a straight line before leaving the road.** For some reason, the drivers simply did not understand the problem or sense of the crisis in time to do anything about it, and just drove off the road. In these straight-crash conditions, the drivers had various options of action, but instead did nothing. Meaning, more than likely, that the driver didn't have a clue as to either what was happening, or how to get out of danger.

Some conditions are more conducive to single-car crashes. Most happen:

- On slippery roads

- On curves

- On 55 mph roads

Statistics reveal that slippery conditions cause 45.8 percent of all single-car accidents meaning that 54.2 percent of all single-car accidents take place on dry roads. Interestingly, **78.7 percent of all accidents happen on dry roads**. Just what causes a no-control situation? Many complex factors affect loss of control of a vehicle. Generally, however, the no-control situation is induced by the driver.

Quite simply, the vehicle does not act in the manner to which the driver is accustomed. Usually, this happens when the driver over controls the car. **Over control** can take several forms, among them:

- **Turning the steering wheel too much**
- **Applying the brakes too hard**
- **Stepping on the gas pedal too hard causing the rear wheels to spin resulting in loss of control**
- **A combination of the above**

In any of these actions, the driver has put a demand on the vehicle that it cannot accept. If the vehicle cannot accept the demands, the vehicle goes out of control.

Accident-Producing Situations Caused by Drivers

Here are some examples of accident-producing situations that drivers get themselves into through their own fault:

- **Tailgating.** Driving to close to the vehicle in front of you. When you do this, you won't have time to react if the other driver brakes, or if there is some other type of emergency.

- **Making a sudden lane change, or a sudden change in speed.** All lane changing should be done as slowly as possible and by giving everyone around you plenty of warning that you are about to make a move.

Admit it. You're often annoyed by drivers who zip from lane to lane, maneuvering about the highway as if they're the only ones on the road. So, don't do the same thing yourself! Train yourself to never make a move with your car without first looking to see if someone is in the space you want to be in. And signal in plenty of time before you make that move.

• **Failure to recognize when you are in trouble.** This is one of the toughest problems you'll face. There's not much you can do to train for this situation, because by the time you know you're in it, you may not be able to get out of it. The best thing for you to do is understand the different situations that can get you into trouble and be able to recognize them before they're inescapable.

• **Not paying attention to the driving task.** Many times this is not because the driver is lazy, but occurs due to drowsiness, stress, and just daydreaming behind the wheel.

• **Driving while emotionally unstable.** Driving while emotionally upset, especially while unusually angry or sad can reduce your ability to recognize danger and avoid it.

Accident-Producing Situations Caused by Vehicle Defects

Very few accidents are caused by a defective vehicle. In modern cars, this sort of catastrophic mechanical failure is practically nonexistent. Unfortunately, while a car may be constructed quite adequately for regular civilian, day-to-day driving, it might not be adequate for emergency drivers.

Almost all vehicle defects give the driver some advance warning that a failure is imminent. Most people ignore the warning signs and keep on driving until there is a dramatic failure of the component or systems. Luckily for these people, when the component or system does finally fail, the worst thing that generally happens is that the car stops and they have to wait for a tow-truck.

Worn tires mean less adhesion with the road and can turn an escapable scenario into an accident. They are the most important component on the car. Badly worn tires can blow out and cause you to lose control of your vehicle. They are even more likely to blow out if the vehicle is driven fast on a hot day.

Photo © Bert Folsom

Tire defects

Tires are better than ever. Today's tires are state-of-the-art. But like any mechanical device, a tire will fail if not well treated. Suffice it to say that it's foolish to drive on badly worn tires.

Keep your windshield, headlights, mirrors and rear window clean. Photo © 2011 Kelpfish/dreamstime

Brake defects

Don't wait until you have to toss out an anchor to stop the car, or until you can hear a metal-to-metal scraping when you hit the brakes. At the first sign of something unusual, have the brakes checked.

Vision restrictions

It is truly amazing to see the number of people that drive around with their windshields and rear windows completely covered with dirt. In order to drive, you have to see where you're going. Take the time to clean all your windows, and make sure the windshield wipers are in good working order. (See *Windshields and Mirrors* chapter, for tips on keeping your windshield and windshield wipers at their best.)

Accident scene Photo © John Foster/Dreamstime

CHAPTER 24

Typical Accident Scenarios and How to Deal with Them

It's impossible to cover all the dangerous situations you can find yourself in when you're driving a car. But a level-headed, quick-reacting defensive driver can do many things to avoid collisions and respond safely:

- **Many times you can avoid a collision by slowing down.**
- Even after it is too late to stop or slow down, **you may often avoid a collision by swerving to one side. It is normally safer to swerve to the right than to the left.**
- **It is better to run off the road to the right than to collide head on.** However, a speeding vehicle cannot be turned sharply without the risk of turning over. The faster a vehicle is going, the more distance it takes to turn safely from a straight path. **Many dangerous situations can be avoided by simply being more alert.**

*Sections in this chapter marked with * are copyright Shell Oil Company material and are reproduced with permission. Material was written by Mike Carpenter and in cooperation with the National Safety Council.*

Yielding Right of Way

A lot of accidents can be avoided if all drivers followed the rules of yielding the right of way. Always observe the rules of right-of-way with judgment and courtesy. Safe drivers give the right-of-way rather than taking it — even if the right of way is legally theirs.

- **In general**, when two vehicles enter an intersection at about the same time, **the vehicle on the left yields the right-of-way to the vehicle on the right.**
- **Always yield right-of-way to the first vehicle arriving at an intersection.**
- When entering a through highway from a secondary road, **give the right-of-way to traffic on the main thoroughfare.**
- **Fire, police, and emergency vehicles have the right-of-way over all other vehicles.**

ACCIDENT SITUATIONS AND HOW TO AVOID THEM

One of the basic points about avoiding accidents is easy to understand and very fundamental to safe driving: **Leave yourself an out. Consider an escape route to every move you make.**

To do this, you have to **be aware of what's going on around you all the time.** Your best tools to avoid accidents are your mirrors–both rearview and side view.

Too many of us only use our rearview mirrors when we want to pull out into traffic. But, in order to see the big picture--accurate information about what's going on you need to view all your mirrors. In an emergency situation, such as a collision on the road ahead, you need all the information you can get about what's happening around you, and you need it fast. **Mirrors are your best way of getting this information.**

Avoiding head-on collisions

Cars may cross the center line and into your intended line of travel while making a left turn or while passing another vehicle. Even on freeways, where most drivers consider themselves safe from oncoming hazards, cars can cross medians or even jump guardrails. The results are head-on crashes.

> **If you see a car coming at you in what looks like it will be a head-on situation, your options are to change speed and/or change direction.**

The best alternative is to slow down and turn to the right. It is far better to go off the road than to hit another vehicle head on. While you're moving to the right, blow your horn, use of; to alert oncoming car. Of course, you must be aware of what you're turning into. **If the right side of the road is occupied by kids getting off a school bus, you really don't have much choice your only alternative is to hit the car.**

If you must move to the left, remember that there's the chance that the oncoming driver might correct at the last minute and turn back into the direction you've just gone. **If you can't avoid a collision, brake firmly and steadily. Every mile per hour you slow down will reduce the impact.**

Accidents while entering the highway or merging

In these situations, cars can squeeze into your path of travel at a slight angle from either side often accelerating from a standing or moving position. They may be changing lanes, or starting out from a parked position along the roadside.

Entering and merging is a common freeway occurrence, where cars merge from ramps and acceleration lanes. **The major problem with the merging car is when it comes equipped with a driver that acts without looking.** In this, as in all driving problems, there is no simple solution to the driver who acts and then looks.

The only solution to this in the entering and merging scenario is to make sure the other driver sees you. Be especially wary of drivers who pull away from parking spaces without looking.

The best way to avoid this on a multi-lane street is to try to stay in the middle or left lane. Otherwise, keep an eye peeled for parked cars with their front wheels canted in toward the street, and that have their brake lights on. They're probably getting ready to pull out and may be in such a hurry they don't bother to look before they move.

Avoiding collisions with cars going in the same direction

Ongoing cars (that is, cars traveling in the same direction and at roughly the same speed you are) cause problems in two basic ways.

The driver of the car ahead of you may suddenly stop or swerve out of the lane to avoid hitting another vehicle or object in the roadway. **Either move on the other car's part can produce a collision.**

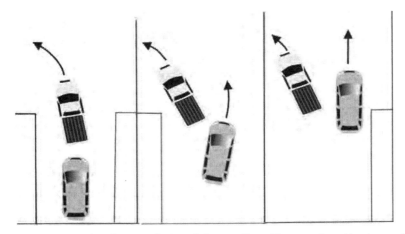

Avoiding a Car Stopped at an Intersection. The car ahead is stopped to make a left turn onto the main road. After pulling ahead somewhat, the driver of the car ahead slams on the brakes. Stop quickly if you can. If not, steer to the car's right. Do not try to pass the other car; it may lead you into the path of oncoming cars that you cannot see.

Drawing and caption courtesy of *Medical Economics*.

- Give the car ahead of you enough room to maneuver.
- Do not tailgate.

Two special situations arise when you are stopped at an intersection.

- You are the first car stopped at an intersection (with or without a stop sign).
- You're waiting to make a left turn. **Keep your front wheels pointed straight until it's time to make that turn.**

Why? Simple. If your wheels are turned left, and you're hit from the rear, your car will be pushed to the left because of the direction the front wheels are pointed. This move would put you directly in the path of oncoming traffic, with the potential of more collisions even more dangerous than the first.

You're the second car in line stopped at an intersection that has a stop sign. The car in front of you pulls out. You look left and right for opposing traffic. It looks OK and you start to pull out, only to find that the driver in front of you has developed cold feet and stopped. You hit him from the rear. In this situation, patience is the key.

Let the first car pull out and clear the intersection, then look both ways to see if it's safe for you to proceed. (See Figure above)

Cars following too closely

A car following you too closely, or closing in on you from behind at a high rate of speed, can crash into your vehicle's rear end should you need to stop suddenly. Tailgaters are always a serious problem, a problem made even worse at night. Fortunately, the solution to a tailgater is not too difficult, pull over and let the idiot go by.

Cars Backing Out

In an urban environment, people are prone to backing out of parking spaces without looking to see what's there. If they are heading toward you, a gentle toot on your horn will inform them that you are there and you'd greatly appreciate it if they would not back into you.

Flying Retreads

If confronted with flying tire treads – boxes – anything that may fly off of a truck or vehicle, first ensure that there are no vehicles coming up behind you on either side of the vehicle.

You can refer to the chapter that covers how to properly adjust your mirrors. The two things the driver needs to do are **slow down and turn the car away from the debris.** Apply the brakes and turn the car away from the obstacle. The most important issue is "look where you want to go". Your hands will follow your eyes. Keep in mind that speed is the issue – if you're going too fast and the debris is too close it will be a difficult maneuver.

Motorcycles and Scooters

Any time you see or hear a motorcycle or scooter near you, be especially cautious. They are difficult to see because they're smaller than most vehicles. **Statistics show that motorcyclists are about 16 times as likely as automobile occupants to die in a traffic crash.**

Pedestrians and bicyclists

Vehicles aren't your only problem. **Pedestrians and bicyclists are potential challenges to your driving skills as well.** Intersecting pedestrian or bicyclist and vehicular traffic is a source of serious problems, despite the many

Cyclists should wear reflective clothing or have reflectors on the bike when venturing out after sunset.   Photo © Mushisushi /dreamstime

control devices used to regulate their interaction. **Intersections are the sites for a very high percentage of all collisions including vehicles, pedestrians, and bicyclists.** Moreover, pedestrians and bicyclists can come into your line of travel at almost any time.

In general, when you pull up to an intersection, always look for conflicting traffic entering— vehicular, pedestrian, and bicyclist. **Even if you have the legal right of way; accident situations, it doesn't protect you from the physical reality of getting hit by a car whose driver just didn't see it your way, or your hitting a pedestrian who decided to cross the street without looking.**

In such situations you will probably not have enough room or time to stop your car. Therefore, you will need to know how to swerve out of harm's way and stop as quickly as possible.

Although many bicyclists have experience riding in traffic and know how to watch out for cars and trucks, many motorists are NOT generally accustomed to bicyclists (and often pedestrians)on the road.

118

Motorists should therefore learn how pedestrians and bicyclists are required to use the road and how to share the road with them courteously and safely.

The following tips for motorists on how to share the road with bicyclists and pedestrians are provided courtesy of Bike Florida and Florida's Share the Road Campaign, Lyndy Lyle Moore, www.bikeflorida.org.

Rules for bicyclists and pedestrians

Bicyclists must obey the same traffic rules and regulations as motor vehicle drivers. This means they ride with traffic (not facing it), and signal, make turns, and stop as any motor vehicle must.

A bicyclist may ride on a sidewalk unless *forbidden by local laws* –this means than in many areas bicyclists MUST use the same road as motorists.

- **Between sunset and sunrise** bicyclists are supposed to have a white light on the front and a red reflector and a red light on the rear.
- **Unlike bicyclists**, pedestrians should walk facing traffic at the edge of the road when there is no sidewalk present.
- **Pedestrians should be visible at night** by wearing bright reflective clothing and carrying a flashlight.
- **Pedestrians should look in all directions** before stepping into the road, even at signalized crosswalks.
- **Pedestrians should be predictable** and cross directly from curb to curb, staying within the marked area or a straight pathway.

Because not all pedestrians and bicyclists (or drivers) follow the rules and regulations perfectly all the time, **motorists must ALWAYS be prepared for the unexpected.** People don't always do what you expect them to do!

- **Slow down in school zones, parks, and residential areas** that are very likely to have pedestrians and/or bicyclists in the roadway).
- **Use extra caution during peak morning and afternoon riding hours.**
- When turning at an intersection with or without a signal, **look for pedestrians and bicyclists crossing from all directions.**

- **Yield to bicyclists and pedestrians** at both marked and un-marked crosswalks–especially when turning right on red.

- **Stop behind the stop bar at intersections, not in the cross-walk,** so pedestrians can cross the street safely.

- Even though a bicyclist's pace may pose a momentary delay in your schedule, **it is important to respect the bicyclist's safety and legal right to the roadways.**

- **Bicyclists' skills vary.** When possible, assess the rider's abilities. A safe, experienced rider holds a steady line.

- **Yield the right of way to a bicyclist as you would a car.**

- **Keep cool, lay off the horn and don't flash your headlights.** It's sometimes OK for a short "toot" to warn bicyclists, but do not BLAST your horn when approaching them--you could startle them and cause them to swerve or fall.

- **When passing bicyclists, reduce speed** and allow three to five feet of passing space between your vehicle and the bicycle. Add one foot for every 10 mph over 50 mph.

A moving vehicle creates wind turbulence that can seriously affect a bicyclist's control. When meeting or passing cyclists, slow down and give the widest berth possible. Crosswinds compound the problem for bicyclists.

Bicyclists worry about road defects you'd never feel in your car. Allow them plenty of room in case they swerve to miss a pothole, storm drain, debris, or other obstacles.

Bicyclists require extra courtesy while on railroad tracks and narrow bridges.

- On a two-lane road, don't pass a bicycle if oncoming traffic is near.

- One Road, Many Users – Be Courteous and share the road.

OTHER DRIVING DANGERS

Accident Situations

Someone Runs a Red Light

Never assume a green light means all okay. There's little consolation in know-ing an accident isn't your fault just because you had the right of way. Your car is still damaged, and someone may be hurt. Even though you were in the right, perhaps you could have actually avoided the collision simply by looking around before you leaped.

- **If your light is green**, make sure cars, at or near the intersection aren't trying to beat the yellow, or red light they are facing.
- **If you're at an intersection without a light**, look left, right, and left again before moving out.

Blowouts

If you slam on the brakes you could lose control. If a front tire blows, the car will pull hard to the side of the blowout. The steering wheel vibrates like crazy.

- **Hang on tight** with your hands at the 9 o'clock and 3 o'clock positions on the steering wheel.
- **Take your foot off the gas** and concentrate on staying in your lane.
- Slow down gradually and **pull off the road to a safe location.**

If a rear tire blows, the back of the car will weave back and forth and vibrate. But you should handle it the same way as you would if a front tire blows.

You Start to Skid

A lot of people hit the brakes hard when their car starts to skid. That generally makes things worse. See "Losing and Regaining Traction" for a thorough discussion of the different kinds of skids and how to handle them.) In general Just take your foot off the gas and turn your steering wheel in the direction you want the front of the car to go. This helps straighten out the car and often regains traction. Frequently it takes more than one turn of the steering wheel to correct a skid.

Brake Failure

You must think and act quickly. Remember
this word-sequence: pump pedal, parking brake, shift down, safe place.

- **Pump the brake pedal.** Sometimes the pressure comes back. (Unless you have an ABS brake system. **Never pump the brake pedal on ABS brakes.**
- **Slowly try the parking brake,** but don't jam it on hard if you're in a curve. That could cause a spin.
- **Shift into a lower gear or lower range** on automatic transmissions. The drag on the engine will help slow you down. Do all three of these as quickly and steadily as you can.

If your car goes into deep water, open windows as fast as possible.
Photo © Zafon/Dreamstime.com

- **Keep your eyes on the road.**
- **Look for a safe place to guide your vehicle onto the shoulder** of the road or some other safe location. In an emergency, the quicker you think and act, the safer you'll be.

Your accelerator gets stuck

- **Try pulling it up with the toe of your shoe.** If a passenger is with you, have him reach down and pull it up. Do not take your eyes off the road to reach down yourself.

- **If your car has a manual transmission,** press down on the clutch. The engine will race, but you can then pull safely off the road.

- **If it's an automatic transmission,** put it in neutral. It's not a good idea to turn off the key. Some cars will lose power steering or even lock the steering wheel.

Your Hood Flies Open

You need to stop, but if you slam on your brakes, you could be hit from behind.

- **In some cars,** from behind the wheel you can actually see ahead by peeking through the opening between the dashboard and the hood.

- If not, then **lean out the window** to see what's ahead of you.

- **In either case,** slow down smoothly and pull off the road.

Your Car Goes Into Deep Water

This doesn't happen often, but it happens enough that you should know what to do.

- **If you do go in the water, release your seat belts immediately.** (But don't release it before you go in. The safety belt will help protect you during impact with the water.)

- **Then the best thing to do is to try to get out quickly through the window**, because power windows can short-circuit in the water.

- **If you can't get out through the window,** try the door. At first, the water pressure will probably hold it closed. But don't panic. As the water rises in the car, it will equalize the pressure and the door should open.

CHAPTER 25

Crash Course

First aid and rescue—Simple Tips that Could

Help Save Lives*

This chapter contains general recommendations that we believe will be helpful in many emergencies. Since every emergency is different, the individual driver must decide what to do in any particular case.

Initial response, I've just seen a bad collision. What can I do to help? *First and foremost, don't make things worse.*

1. **Pass well beyond the wreck before signaling and pulling off of the road,** out of harm's way. This keeps you from blocking the view of the collision to oncoming traffic, and it gives emergency crews room to work.

2. **Turn on your emergency flashers and raise your hood** to call attention to yourself.

3. Then **carefully approach the wreck**, avoiding dangerous situations like wires, fires or hazardous materials.

4. Next, **turn off the ignitions of all vehicles** to reduce the risk of fire. This simple step could keep a bad collision from becoming much worse. Remember, check for spilled gasoline or downed power lines before getting too close. And don't move an injured driver to get to his keys.

5. Now **call for help if possible**. Be sure to stay on the line until the emergency dispatcher hangs up. If you're needed to administer first aid, assign the call to someone else and be specific: "You in the red jacket call 9-1-1!"

6. **Consider carrying a cellular phone in your car.** Many of today's models have emergency numbers programmed into them.

7. **Check for injuries.** Are victims awake and responsive? If so, encourage them not to move. If they don't respond, verify that they are breathing. Then attend to those with severe bleeding (wear latex gloves if possible).

Copyright, 2011 Shell Oil Company. Material reproduced with permission. Written in cooperation with the National Safety Council and the American Trauma Society. Hands-Only CPR material courtesy of the American Red Cross. Additional material from Anita Liggett, RN, CPR instructor for the American Heart Association.

Check to see if the victims are awake and responsive.

NEVER MOVE A VICTIM UNLESS THERE IS AN IMMEDIATE, LIFE-THREATENING DANGER SUCH AS FIRE, LEAKING FUEL, OR RISING WATER.

Should I always stop?

Whatever the situation, your intervention might help save a life. Wouldn't you want to be helped if you were the one trapped or injured?

Also, if you were involved in the collision, you must stop. All states impose severe penalties on drivers who don't stop in such cases. Remember, you can be involved in a collision without actually hitting anything. If you contribute to a crash in any way, you're obligated to stop.

If the fear of making a mistake keeps you from stopping, be aware that most states have first aid and rescue Good Samaritan laws to protect individuals from liability if they stop and, in good faith, administer first aid. The scope of protection varies, so check your state's laws.

IF EMERGENCY CREWS ARE RACING TO A CRASH AHEAD OF YOU, pull over to let them safely pass. And don't assume the first ambulance or police car you see will be the only one. Watch for other emergency vehicles following closely behind the first. The last thing you want to do is pull out and cause another collision.

Evaluating the injured.

What's my first step in treating the injured?

Before beginning any first aid, check to see if any victims are awake and responsive. This may help you assess the level of care each victim needs.

A conscious victim's responses will often help you evaluate the extent of his injuries. What hurts? may reveal broken bones, bleeding or internal injuries. Can you wiggle your fingers or toes? could help you assess potential spinal damage. *And no response at all might mean a victim isn't breathing.*

Breathing and artificial respiration

I don't think she's breathing! Now what?

- **First, make sure breathing has stopped.** Is the victim completely non-responsive? Is her/his chest rising and falling? Can you feel breathing? Hear it? If the victim is not breathing, open her airway. Gently move the head into its normal, eyes front position and lower the jaw.
- **Listen for gurgling or gagging.** Both are signs of a blocked airway. If you hear either after opening the mouth, gently clear it of any obstructions.
- **If the victim is still not breathing, begin artificial respiration.** Pinch the victim's nose shut. Open your mouth wide, take a deep breath, and put your mouth tightly over the victim's (you may wish to carry a pocket mask or mouth barrier for such emergencies). Blow a full breath, then watch for the victim's chest to rise and fall. If she doesn't start breathing on her own, blow one full breath every five seconds. Do this for at least one minute. **Be sure to breathe yourself— you don't want to hyperventilate!**

The person collapsed in front of me. Should I perform CPR.

The American Red Cross offers courses in **Hands-Only CPR** for witnessed sudden collapse. Contact your local Red Cross chapter for classes. Visit www.redcross.org. for locations.

Hands-only CPR is a potentially lifesaving technique involving no mouth to mouth contact. It is best used in emergencies where someone has seen another person suddenly collapse. The hands-only technique increases the likelihood of surviving cardiac emergencies that occur outside medical settings.

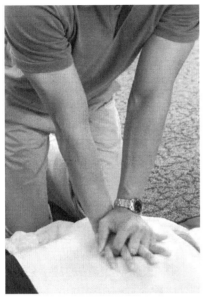

Hands-Only CPR
Photo © American Heart Association

American Heart Association studies show that "Chest compression-only CPR, also known as hands-only CPR, has been shown in studies to be at least as effective as standard CPR with mouth-to-mouth ventilation for adult primary cardiac arrest victims," Bobrow said. "And because of its simplicity, hands-only CPR may be quicker and easier for lay rescuers to learn, remember and perform than conventional CPR."

The Hands-Only CPR procedure

For witnessed sudden collapse

Check and Call

• Check the scene, then check the person

• Tap on the shoulder and shout, "Are you okay?" And quickly look for breathing.

• Call 9-1-1 if no response.

If unresponsive and not breathing, begin chest compressions.

Tips

• Whenever possible, use disposable gloves when giving care.

• Occasional gasps are not "breathing."

• **DO NOT STOP** Except in one of these situations:

• You see an obvious sign of life (breathing).

• Another trained responder arrives and takes over.

• EMS personnel arrive and takes over.

• You are too exhausted to continue.

• An AED (Automated External Defibrillator is ready to use.

• The scene becomes unsafe.

GIVE CHEST COMPRESSIONS

1. Place the heel of one hand on the center of the chest.

2. Place the heel of the other hand on top of the fist hand, lacing your fingers together.

3. Keep your arms straight, position your shoulders directly over your hands.

4. Push hard, push fast.

5. Compress the chest at least two 2 inches.

6. Compress at least 100 times per minute.

7. Let the chest rise completely before pushing down again.

8. Continue chest compressions.

An air ambulance is used where either a traditional ambulance cannot reach the scene easily or quickly enough, or the patient needs to be transported over a distance or terrain that makes air transportation the most practical.

If an AED is available

1. Turn on AED

2. Wipe chest dry

3. Attach the pads.

4. Plug in connector, if necessary.

5. Make sure on one is touching the individual.

6. Push the "Analyze" button, if necessary

7. If a shock is advised, push the "shock" button.

8. Perform compressions and follow AED prompts.

An AED or automated external defibrillator is a portable electronic device that automatically diagnoses life threatening cardiac arrhythmias and is able to treat them through electrical therapy. The use of AEDs is taught in many first aid, first responder, and basic life support (BLS) level CPR classes.

COURSES

American Red Cross. Go to **redcross.org** or call your local chapter to sign up for training in full CPR, Pet First Aid and much more.

Additional training is offered by the **American Heart Association**. Hands OnlyTM CPR: http://handsonlycpr.org/.

2010 Guidelines for CPR and Emergency Cardiovascular Care: www.heart.org/cprguidelines.

Video training as brief as one minute led to participants being more likely to give hands-only CPR, at a rate and compression depth significantly closer to the ideal than those with no training.

Hands OnlyTM CPR video demonstration: www.youtube.com/watch?v=zuJkRpJ7Fxg&feature=relmfu.

How do I control severe bleeding.

- **Press firmly against any wounds with some sort of bandage, preferably a thick pad of clean cloth.** This will absorb the blood and allow it to clot. (If possible, place a barrier-- several layers of cloth, latex gloves, a plastic bag between you and the victim's blood.)

If blood soaks through the dressing, don't remove it. That could open

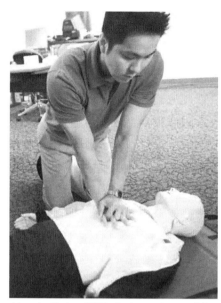

Hands-Only CPR trainee tests his skill on a practice dummy.
Courtesy of the American Heart Association

the wound further and make bleeding worse. Instead, add more layers of cloth and apply pressure even more firmly. If possible, get someone else at the scene to help you tie the bandage in place.

If the bleeding still won't stop, make sure you're pressing on the right spot. **It's not a good idea to use your belt as a tourniquet.** That might completely cut off the flow of blood, and could potentially lead to the loss of the limb.

Should I be worried about AIDS

The American Medical Association reports that **it is extremely unlikely that you will contract AIDS** from a bleeding collision victim, or from mouth-to-mouth contact during artificial respiration.

The HIV virus, which causes AIDS, is transmitted through sexual contact, infected blood, infected needles or childbirth, and not through casual contact.

Still, you may want to **stock your glove compartment with a Laerdal™ Pocket CPR Mask to avoid direct contact.** They are available from the Red Cross store online at www.redcrossstore.org or your local chapter store. Prices range from $2.50 US for a Keychain mini CPR mask to about $12.95 for an entire kit. They are also available at www.crp-savers.com and www.amazon.com. You may also want to keep several pairs of latex gloves in your first aid kit (freezer bags are a good substitute).

If I have to move someone, how should I do it?

- Remember, you should only **move a crash victim when there is an immediate danger, such as fire or rising water.**
- If you must move a victim, gently align his neck and spine. Then, if you are alone, carefully drag him backward by the clothes or armpits. **Do not pull a victim sideways, as this will only aggravate spinal damage.**

• If you have help available, have one person support the head from underneath, keeping it in line with the spine. The others can then lift the body from the sides, evenly supporting it from underneath.

I think the victim is in shock. Now what?

Shock occurs when a victim's circulatory system doesn't provide enough blood to his body and brain.

Shock can kill, know how to recognize it – shock victims often walk, talk and at first *seem merely shaken up*. **Telltale signs** include pale, moist, clammy skin; dilated pupils; a weak and rapid pulse; shivering, thirst, nausea and vomiting, shallow breathing, weakness, a vacant expression and a detached attitude.

Be ready to perform CPR with the American Red Cross CPR Key chain with Gloves. The kit includes a one-way valve breathing barrier that protects the rescuer by preventing direct contact with the patient's mouth. A printed illustration to indicate correct use is inside.

- **If you suspect an apparently uninjured victim is in shock,** have her (or him) lie down and raise her feet slightly.
- It's generally best to **place blankets and coats under her and around her** to conserve heat.
- **If the victim is nauseated**, have her lie on her side and slightly elevate her head.
- Then **begin any additional first aid, talking to the victim as you work.** A little kindness and understanding go a long way toward treating shock

If You're in an Accident

How can I help myself if I'm in a wreck?

If it's a minor collision with no injuries, you can best help yourself by staying calm and moving out of traffic. The key here is safety first, insurance later. Keep a pad and pencil handy, and use them, along with insurance forms, to exchange information once you have cleared the scene.

If you're in a major collision, you'll have to be the judge of whether or not you are injured and how quickly traffic is moving around you. Often, your best bet is to wait for help from a safe place which just might be your car. If you're uninjured and traffic permits, you may want to begin first aid on those around you. But don't put yourself at more risk doing so. You'll be no help to anyone if you lapse into shock or get struck by a passing motorist.

The Glove Compartment and Trunk

Keep Them Well Stocked for Safety

What to have on hand for roadside emergencies.

1. First aid kit - It should includes bandages, antibiotic ointments, gauzes, aspirin, and sanitary wipes.

2. Blanket – to warm a passenger or driver who goes into shock or is chilled.

3. Road flairs – these traffic signalers make oncoming traffic vehicles aware of your accident situation and to steer clear of the accident site.

4. Reflective triangle – these can be placed on the road as an indicator like the road flairs

5. Disposable camera – or a smart phone with a built in cameras. Record vehicle damage, the scene of the accident, and any injuries for insurance purposes.

6. Pen and paper – To jot down information you may need from the other driver(s), the police, and/or witnesses.

7. Bottled water and energy bar –Stay as hydrated and alert as possible.

8. Cellular phone – Crucial to contact police and medical services.

9. Emergency contact numbers – Keep a list of emergency contact numbers stored in your car or cell phone or written out in the glove compartment

10. Hammer to break the window if needed. Auto stores and departments often carry small, pointed hammers for use in cars.

11. CPR mask, pocket mask or keychain mini mask. Available from www.redcrossstore.org

Chapter 26

SAFETY FEATURES
Seat Belts and Air Bags

SEAT BELTS

The facts are in on seat belts: **THEY SAVE LIVES**. Plain and simple. People have sometimes questioned the use of seat belts, expressing fears that belts could get in the way of fast exits from the car. But by not wearing a seat belt, you could experience a faster and deadly exit—right through the windshield or a flung-open door.

Even in a minor fender-bender you could be bounced around severely inside the car. And just think about what would happen in a rollover.

THERE IS NO EXCUSE FOR NOT WEARING A SEAT BELT!

Why Do We Need Seat Belts?

Its amazing that even some driving professionals ask that question when the answer is so obvious. Sure, we all know the story of the guy who didn't wear a belt and was tossed free of the car in the accident when the car blew up and became an inferno. That guy must be the most popular man in the world because everybody knows him. Stop and think about this story. **Can you imagine what it would be like to be thrown free or jump out of a car that was moving along at 40 mph?** It could ruin your whole day. Along with your face, and most of what's attached to it.

Wearing a seat belt is merely a recognition of Sir Isaac Newton's Laws of Motion. Objects at rest tend to stay that way; likewise, moving objects tend to keep moving. A large, stationary object, such as a roadside telephone pole or tree, wants to stay that way. Your car, traveling towards that stationary object, wants to keep moving. When the stationary and the moving meet, something has to give. Generally, those *somethings* are you and your car.

When your car hits the pole, it stops. Unfortunately, unless you are secured to the car by a seat belt, you don't stop moving. You travel forward to meet and sometimes go through the windshield. Seat belts are designed to keep this from happening.

Rollover crashes can be particularly injurious to vehicle occupants because of the unpredictable motion of the vehicle. In a rollover crash, unbelted occupants can be thrown against the interior of the vehicle and strike hard surfaces such as steering wheels, windows and other interior components. They also have a great risk of being ejected, which usually results in very serious injuries. Ejected occupants also can be struck by their own or other vehicles.

How to Wear a Seat Belt Properly

If your seat belt is uncomfortable, you're probably not wearing it properly. A lot of people complain that seat belts are uncomfortable and many people don't wear them for that reason. Try wearing a neck brace or spending a few weeks in traction. You'll really know what discomfort is.

If you're experiencing chafing on your shoulder, try a cushioned seat belt wrap available in auto part shops and automotive departments of department stores. They wrap around the belt with Velcro. If you can't find any, a folded wash cloth between your skin and the seat belt may be helpful.

Belts should be worn so there is none of the slack that allows the body to move forward before being stopped by the belt. In a severe collision, a too-loose belt might produce bruises, but bruises are far better than having your face introduced to the windshield.

The lap portion of the belt should be comfortable but tight.

The buckle should never be over your stomach. It should be at your side, on the hip.

Most cars today have inertia-reel seat belts that allow passengers and drivers freedom of movement inside the car, while retaining the ability to lock in place when sudden tension, such as that encountered in a sudden stop or collision, takes place.

Where mandatory seat belt laws are in effect, automobile fatalities have gone down. That is not speculation. That is fact.

If you're going to be a responsible, safe driver, you must take responsibility for the safety of your passengers as well as yourself. Make sure all adults wear their seat belts and that all children are secured in child safety seats.

CHILD SAFETY SEATS

For Short Trips, Why Bother with a Child Safety Seat?

The greatest number of crashes occur on short trips at low speeds. Three-fourths of all crashes happen within 25 miles of home. And 40% of all fatal crashes take place on roads where the speed limit is 45 mph or less.

THINK OF A CHILD SAFETY SEAT AS A LIFE PRESERVER.

An Adults Lap Is Pretty Safe, Right?

Wrong. Grown-up arms are no substitute for a safety restraint. In a 30-mph crash, a child is thrown forward with a force equal to 20 times his or her weight. Plus, if the adult is not wearing a safety belt, the child could get crushed between the adult and the windshield or dashboard.

When Are Kids Big Enough for a Regular Seat Belt?

- In general, **when they're over 80 pounds and approximately eight years of age.** Too many children start using regular belts too soon. Your child has a proper fit when:
- **The lap belt stays** low and snug across the hips without riding up over the stomach.
- **The shoulder belt** does not cross the face or front of the neck.

There Are So Many Kinds of Safety Seats. Which One Is Best?

- The best child safety seat is the one that fits the child, fits the vehicle, and can be installed and used correctly every time.

There are three basic types:

1. Rear-facing infant seats are designed for babies from birth until at least 20 pounds and one year of age. Rear-facing infant car seats are small and portable and fit newborns best. Don't confuse them with infant carriers.

2. Convertible safety seats convert from rear-facing to forward-facing for toddlers between one and four years of age, who weigh between 20 and 40 pounds. Convertible seats are used rear-facing for infants and forward-facing for toddlers.

3. Booster seats are used as a transition to safety belts by older kids who have clearly outgrown their convertible seat but are not quite ready for the vehicles belt system. A booster seat raises the child so that the lap and shoulder belts fit properly. If your car only has lap belts, use a shield booster. IN ALL CASES, check your owners manual and car seat instructions to see if you need a locking clip to help secure the child's seat. It comes with all seats.

Why Does an Infant Seat Have to Face the Rear?

Babies need the extra protection provided by the back of the safety seat, which absorbs and spreads the force of the crash. The infant's neck muscles are weak. If the baby faces forward, the head could snap forward in a crash, risking serious injury to the neck and spinal cord.

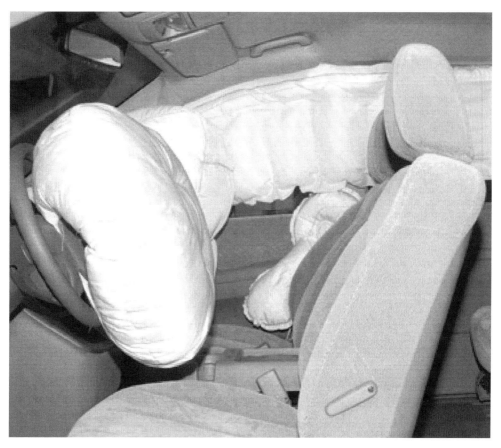

Front, side and curtain air bags protect driver and front seat passenger in this vehicle.

Never Put a Rear-Facing Infant Seat in the Front when there's a Passenger Air Bag.

Air bags inflate at speeds up to 200 mph!
A safety seat in the front puts the child too close to the bag when its inflating and can cause serious injury or death.

How Do I Make Sure the Child Safety Seat Is Working?

Always read the instructions that come with a child safety seat (keeping them handy at all times), and read all sections in your vehicle owners manual that discuss safety seat installation. This is especially important because many child safety seats and vehicle belt systems are not compatible.

Children are properly restrained only when:

The child fits securely in the safety seat, AND The safety seat itself fits securely in the vehicle seat. If it doesn't, contact the safety seat manufacturer.

Don't forget to mail in the registration card that comes with a new seat. Then the manufacture can let you know of any problems or recalls.

Where's the Safest Place for Kids in the Car?

The back seat is the safest place for a child of any age. And the safest place in the back seat is in the center if you have center belts and an appropriate vehicle seat. The most distance from impact usually means the most protection. In the back, the child is farther away from the impact of a head-on collision, which can cause the most serious injuries. Just as important, the child is safely removed from the passenger air bag.

Photo © Paul Hakimata, Dreamstime

I'm Not Comfortable with My Child in the Back. Shouldn't She Be Closer to Me?

No. The back seat is the safest. It may help to compare your child in the back to when your child is home sleeping. You probably don't feel the need to be right next to your baby all through the night or during a nap. A healthy baby properly secured in a safety seat should not need constant watching.

If a child in the back does need attention, don't try any one-hand-on-the-wheel maneuvers. Just pull over.

If an Older Child Must Be Seated in Front . . .

If an older child must be seated in front, make sure he or she is correctly retrained for age and size and always slide the vehicle seat as far back as possible to put maximum distance between the child and an air bag.

Side and curtain air bags in this Mercedes deploy in the front and rear seats. Photo courtesy of Mercedes-Benz, North America.

Air Bags

Air bags inflate when the crash forces are about equivalent to striking a brick wall head-on at 10-15 miles per hour or a similar-sized vehicle head-on at 20-30 mph. Standard driver-side and passenger-side air bags are not designed to deploy in side, rear, or rollover crashes.

Since standard driver-side and passenger-side air bags provide supplemental protection only in frontal crashes, safety belts should always be used to provide maximum protection.

Chapter 27
Airbags
How They Work and Precautions to Take

Standard driver-side and passenger-side air bags are designed to save lives and prevent injuries by cushioning vehicle occupants as they move forward in a moderate-to-severe front-end or near front-end crash.

They keep the occupants head, neck, and chest from hitting the steering wheel or dashboard.

Air bags inflate when crash forces are about equivalent to striking a brick wall head-on at 10-15 mph or a similar-sized vehicle head-on at 20-30 mph.

Standard driver-side and passenger-side air bags are not designed to deploy in side, rear, or rollover crashes. (As we will discuss later, however, special side air bags are available for some vehicles.)

Since standard driver-side and passenger-side air bags provide supplemental protection only in frontal crashes, safety belts should always be used to provide maximum protection in rollovers and all crashes.

Check your owners manual to see whether or not your vehicle is equipped with air bags, and whether or not you have a passenger-side air bag.

Check for a warning label on the sun visor and/or the front of the right door frame. A passenger-side air bag is in a compartment in the dash board. The compartment may have a cover labeled SRS (Supplemental Restraint System) or SIR (Supplemental Inflation Restraint).

Since model year 1998, all new passenger cars have dual air bags (driver and passenger side). Starting in model year 1999, all new light trucks have dual air bags. Each vehicle is equipped with a unique air bag which will deploy with a different force.

Driver and passenger air bags fully deployed.
Photo courtesy Mercedes-Benz, North America

HOW AIR BAGS WORK

Air Bag System Components

Most air bag systems consist of three main components:
- An air bag module
- One or more crash sensors
- A diagnostic unit

The air bag module, which contains an inflator and a vented, lightweight fabric air bag, sits in the hub of the steering wheel on the driver side ,and, if the vehicle is so equipped, in the instrument panel (dashboard) on the passenger side.

Crash sensor(s), on the front of the vehicle or in the passenger compartment, measure deceleration the rate at which a vehicle slows down. When these sensors detect rapid decelerations that indicate a crash, they send a signal to the inflator that deploys the bag.

The diagnostic unit monitors the readiness of the air bag system whenever the vehicle ignition is turned on and the engine is running. A warning light on the dashboard will alert the driver if the air bag system needs service.

Once an air bag is deployed, it cannot be reused. Air bag system parts must be replaced by an authorized service dealer for the system to once again be operational.

Rapid Deployment

The entire deployment, inflation, and deflation cycle is over in less than one second.

The bag inflates within about 1/20th of a second after impact. At 1/5th of a second following impact, the air bag begins to deflate and deflates rapidly as the gas escapes through vent holes or through the porous air bag fabric.

Initial deflation enhances the cushioning effect of the air bag by maintaining approximately the same internal pressure as the occupant strikes into the bag.

Rapid deflation enables the driver to maintain control if the vehicle is still moving after the crash, and prevents the driver and/or the right-front passenger from being trapped by the inflated air bag.

Dust

Dust particles present during the inflation cycle come from dry powder used to lubricate the tightly-packed air bag to ease rapid unfolding during deployment. Small amounts of particulate produced from combustion within the inflator also are released as gas is vented from the air bag. These dust particles may produce minor throat and/or eye irritation.

SIDE AND CURTAIN AIR BAGS

Side and curtain air bags fully deployed.
Photo courtesy Mercedes-Benz

A number of auto manufacturers offer side-mounted and curtain-like side air bags which deploy from the roof and may span the entire side of the passenger compartment.

Side air bags protect drivers and front-seat adult passengers in certain side-impact collisions. (A few manufacturers offer side air bags in the rear seat, too.)

Side impact air bags can provide significant safety benefits to adults; however, as with ALL air bags (as we shall see), children seated in close proximity to a side air bag may be at risk of serious or fatal injury, especially if the child's head, neck, or chest is in close proximity to the air bag at the time of deployment.

Because there are variations in the design and performance of side air bags, you should carefully read your owners manual to see if it is safe for children to sit next to the side air bags.

Curtain air bags come down along the window to protect your head and neck. The curtain air bags work in conjunction with side air bags and can prevent both front and rear occupants from hitting their heads on the side windows or roof pillars in a severe side collision. Plus, the air-filled cushion can block glass splinters or other objects that could cause injuries in a side impact or rollover.

Door-mounted air bags break out of the armrest of the door just above the armrest. These protect your chest.

Seat-mounted systems deploy from the side of the seat-back cushion closest to the door. Some inflate to the size of a small pillow, while others can inflate to the size of a large cushion. The smaller ones shield your chest, while the larger ones protect both your head and chest.

PRECAUTIONS TO TAKE

Whether a deploying air bag is an effective lifesaver or a danger itself depends on where and how occupants are seated and restrained in the vehicle.

The Risk Zone

The force of a **deploying air bag** is greatest in the first 2-3 inches after the air bag bursts through its cover and begins to inflate. Those 2-3 inches are the "risk zone."

The force decreases as the air bag inflates further. **Occupants who are very close to, or in contact with, the cover of a stored air bag when the air bag begins to inflate can be hit with enough force to suffer serious injury or death.**

In contrast, **occupants who are properly restrained and who sit 10 inches away from the air bag cover will contact the air bag only after it has completely or almost completely inflated.** The air bag then will cushion and protect them from hitting hard surfaces in the vehicle and thus provide a significant safety benefit, particularly in moderate to serious crashes.

The big danger is contact with or close proximity to the air bag module at the initial instant of deployment.

Air Bag Fatalities

On the driver side, fatally-injured drivers have been those who are believed to have sat close to their steering wheels either by habit or because they couldn't reach the steering wheel or gas and brake pedals if they sat farther back. Some had grown accustomed to sitting close to their steering wheel as matter of a preference.

On the passenger side, it has been primarily children who get too close to the air bag; however, confirmed adult deaths involving passenger-side air bags have also been caused by their proximity to the air bag when it deployed. The most common reason for the adults' proximity was failure to use seat belts.

Most passenger-side air bag fatalities have been infants and young children. Older children killed by frontal air bags were either unbelted or improperly belted and moved too close to the air bag during braking.

Some air bag fatalities have been attributed to the air bags design. As a result, new air bag designs deploy first radially and then toward the occupant. Advanced air bags adjust deployment force or suppress deployment altogether.

Protecting Yourself and Your Passengers from Potential Air Bag Injury

Children

All new cars must have labels placed conspicuously on the sun visors, dashboards, and child restraints to highlight the dangers of placing children in the front seat of vehicles with air bags.

Rear-facing infant car seats place infants in great danger in the front seat because the child's head is too close to the dashboard where the air bag is stored.

Infants in rear-facing car seats in vehicles with passenger-side air bags should NEVER be placed in the front seat. Period.

Older children in the front seat get too close when they are allowed to ride completely unrestrained. During pre-crash braking, these unrestrained children slide forward and are up against or very near the dashboard when the air bag begins to deploy. Because of their proximity, the children can sustain fatal head or neck injuries from the deploying passenger air bag.

Similarly, some children who wear seat belts, but who are really too small to be using just a vehicle lap and shoulder belt, are equally at risk.

So how can you protect children from potential air bag injury?

- To begin with, as discussed in the previous chapter, the best place for children to be seated in a vehicle is in the back seat, preferably in the center (if proper restraints are available in that position, and the children are properly restrained for their age and size.)
- Depending on the size of the child, you should use a booster seat plus a lap/shoulder belt, or a lap/shoulder belt alone (for larger children). The vehicle seat needs to be pushed all the way back, to maximize the distance between the child and the air bag.
- The child needs to be sitting with his/her back against the seat back, not wiggling around or leaning forward, with as little slack as possible in the belt in order to minimize forward movement in a crash.

Adults

Adults sitting in the front passenger seat of a vehicle equipped with a passenger-side air bag should:

- Be properly restrained in a seat belt
- Sit at least 10 inches away from the air bag compartment.

145

- Avoid leaning or reaching forward.
- Remain seated against the vehicle seat back, with as little slack in the belt as possible to minimize forward movement in a crash.

Short adults

Short adults in the front passenger seat of a vehicle equipped with a passenger-side air bag should additionally:
- Move the seat as far rearward as possible.
- Tilt the seat back slightly to help maximize the distance between their chest and the instrument panel (to 10 inches or more).
- Refrain from moving around or sitting on the edge of the seat which could move their head too close to the air bag.

Elderly drivers and passengers

- Elderly people, like all other drivers and front seat passengers, should be properly restrained and should move the seat as far rearward as possible, being careful to remain seated against the vehicle seat back and keeping the arms away from the area in which the air bag will deploy.

Tilt and Telescoping Steering Wheels

- A tilt steering wheel should be tilted down so that the air bag will deploy toward the chest and not the head.
- Pregnant women should make sure the steering wheel is also tilted toward the chest, not the abdomen or the head.
- A telescoping steering wheel should be positioned so that it extends toward the driver as little as possible, ensuring that the air bag has plenty of room to deploy.

Manual On-Off Switches for Air Bags

The **National Highway Traffic Safety Administration allows passenger air bag cut-off switches to be installed in vehicles with no rear seats or small rear seats.** Manufacturers may also use lower-powered air bags, which permits air bags to be de-powered by 20 to 35 percent.

For a copy of the government rules call the AutoSafety HotLine (800-424-9393) or visit the website (http://www.nhtsa.dot.gov).

All written comments/questions concerning air bags should be addressed to the Administrator (NAO-10), NHTSA, 400 Seventh St., SW, Washington, DC 20590.

Vehicle owners may request authorization for a dealer to connect the air bag (driver side, passenger side, or both) to an on-off switch.

Vehicle owners can request an on-off switch by filling out an agency request form and submitting the form to the National Highway Traffic Safety Administration. (Website: www.nhtsa.dot.gov). Since the risk groups for drivers are different from those for passengers, a separate certification must be made on an agency request form for each air bag to be equipped with an on-off switch.

If NHTSA approves a request, the agency will send the owner a letter authorizing the installation of one or more on-off switches in the owners vehicle. The owner may give the authorization letter to any dealer or repair business, which may then install the switch(s).

NEVER ATTEMPT TO DISABLE THE AIR BAG YOURSELF.

An air bag system is highly sophisticated and the air bag deploys with great force. Tampering with an air bag system is very risky. An inadvertent deployment can cause serious injuries. **Once an air bag is deployed, it cannot be reused .**

Rapid Deployment

The entire deployment, inflation, and deflation cycle is over in less than one second. The bag inflates within about 1/20th of a second after impact. At 1/5th of a second following impact, the air bag begins to deflate

Index

E

D

F

Made in the USA
San Bernardino, CA
15 January 2015